T0207954

Essays in Definition

One Man's Search for Meaning

Eston Eugene Roberts

authorHOUSE®

AuthorHouse™
1663 Liberty Drive
Bloomington, IN 47403
www.authorhouse.com
Phone: 1 (800) 839-8640

"Cover Photo Credit to Madelyn Rubin Photography"

Published by AuthorHouse 03/27/2018

ISBN: 978-1-5462-2963-6 (sc)
ISBN: 978-1-5462-2961-2 (hc)
ISBN: 978-1-5462-2962-9 (e)

Library of Congress Control Number: 2018902098

Print information available on the last page.

This book is printed on acid-free paper.

Scripture taken from The Holy Bible, King James Version. Public Domain

Contents

In Memory of Preston James Roberts
1957-2017
Too Soon Departed

[Interior drawings by PJR]

Introduction

*This is a compilation of essays born of varying impetuses and written over a number of years on the general topic of metaphor, my life-obsession since my spring semester at Berry College in 1953. The generalized purpose of the following documents is to trace the path of metaphor as my thinking evolved. More importantly, it is hoped that these essays—read along with my prolix and sometimes confusing opus—my chef d' oeuvre on metaphor, **Metamorphosos: A Proposed Path to Independent Living**—will shed new light on some of the major philosophical conundrums perplexing the world today.*

Among these conundrums, the still unresolved issues growing out of Albert Einstein's relativity theories—one of which is determinism: are we prisoners of our particle origins, consigned to a preordained cycle of macro machinery, or free individuals equipped with the necessary tools to exercise free will and control our destinies?

One reasonable answer to these questions may be found, I believe, in my theory of metaphor.

In the first place (as argued in "Everything is Metaphor" below), metaphor is literally the process of creation, the system whereby everything on the planet, including the planet, is made. Aristotle—denied advantages associated with modern concepts like quantum mechanics—erred when he limited the purview of metaphor to rhetoric. This is because (according to me), since the advent of self-concept, metaphor has been the central factor in every aspect of modern living—from psychology to philosophy, from technology to science.

Another goal of these selected essays is to encourage the habit of serious thinking—what Matthew Arnold termed "high seriousness." I seem to recall a time when intellectual curiosity— fueled by the need to know self and where one existed on the planes of existence—drove people to the reading of literature and the study of ideas and philosophy. That time is threatened now-a-days as denizens of the planet seem to seek instant gratification in intoxicants, the worlds of virtual reality, in games and electronic warfare, in pulp fiction, and the proliferation of fake—that is ungrounded in fact and designed to cuckold—news.

Metaphor rules the world, and one can only conjecture where concepts of self geared by escapism—a form of escapist metaphor based on live-for-the-moment philosophy and other-world activity—will take us.

This brings me to the final point, alluded to above, of this introduction: Metaphors require grounding for effectiveness, and in a real world where survival—physical and psychological—is ultimately based on real-world performance, it is imperative that men and women ground their behavior in responsible actions, actions taken in the best interests of self-concept.

Taken in whole, these essays propose that taking responsibility for the construction of self-concept is the gateway to a world where ecology thrives, where hunger doesn't exist, and where war and every form of prejudice is banished from the planet.

Ultimately, I believe, implementing the philosophy of metaphor as revealed in these essays will lead to that most important desire of the human soul—freedom of the individual to create and enjoy his/her vision of what this spasm of energy called life really means.

The following essay is a product of a summer spent in a log cabin on Rich Mountain in Transylvania County, North Carolina. A debt of gratitude is owed Robert M. Persig and his once-famous work, **Zen and the Art of Motorcycle Maintanance,** *which I read to smithereens. That I ended up rejecting his major premise—Zen Buddhism is a path to passivity—in no way diminishes my immense respect for a man who dared great things and accomplished much.*

The essay comes first in this collection because it represents the initial rendition of the formal concept of metaphor. Over time, the philosophy has metastasized into a world-view and a vision for the eventual enrichment of human kind. It is a proposal, a metaphor; and, as stipulated: No metaphor is right or wrong, just efficient or not.

A Pond, A Mirror, A Metaphor

It was May and it was mountain and it was a tiny cabin beside a tiny pond. I was there to read, to write, to rusticate, to muse.

From the screened-in porch, from my ancient rocker puffing tumid clouds of cotton, I could view on my left the scrambling profusion of "country" roses. Straight ahead lay the shallow, shadowed pond muttering the never-ending mumble of its scanty overflow. It braceleted the four-room cabin. On my right, mirrored perfectly in the water, the pink-white rhododendron blossoms stood and shimmered.

Suddenly I found myself saying aloud—I often talk to myself when really alone—"I prefer the reflected world to the one that's real."

Now anyone who knows anything knows that's insane. You can't eat, touch, or even smell a reflection; and I already said I talk to myself. (If the truth were known, I talk to many things not sentient in the human sense.)

A few summers earlier I talked to an enormous rainbow trout—caught from this very pond—saying, when I saw his coat of many colors, "I'm sorry, boy!" and I talked this summer, several times, to the gray-spotted hawk that swooped across the mist-smoked morning waters. From an oak on my left she considered, by turns, me and the king-fishers that fished the pond rich with salamander but minus, alas, and thanks to me, of fish.

And I talked to the burnished, emerald serpent who had, surreptitiously, deposited his micaceous skin and came, at times, to sun with it upon a slab of concrete beside the chain-link fence. To be honest, these conversations were always one-sided and very brief, he preferring the weeds and fronds beside the pond to me.

I even talked, sometimes blasphemously, to the wasps that—warmed awake by the morning sun—functioned as alarm clock.

Furthermore, I've even been known to carry on a conversation with a hammer that knew a nail when it missed one. (I'm a very talkative fellow when in the right kind of company!) But, still, the conviction that I preferred the reflected world to the real one lingered.

Now, mind you, I'm no Platonist. In fact, I abhor everything the concept stands for. Frozen, a metaphor becomes a trap, an idea made perfect by cryogenics. Spirituality cannot be capped off and sold, like natural gas, for warmth or profit.

But I get ahead of myself. I was saying you can't eat, touch, or even smell a reflection, that talking aloud when you're by yourself isn't quite kosher. Such things can get you tagged by a very potent metaphor—insanity.

So be it.

It was some days later—maybe even June or July (the roses had crumpled into tiny fists by then, but the rhododendron still pulsed metaphors)—when a sudden shower sprinkled the pond with bubbles, erasing my mirrored world. A muttered rumble of thunder accompanied the show, and a line of iambic verse leaped spontaneously into my mind: "The thunder grumbled angrily, disturbed at getting wet."

The more I thought about that line, the more it bugged me. Was it any less a metaphor than what the pond revealed to me? (As the pond is a mind that reflects, subject to light and shadow, what it perceives but not what is, so is a metaphor nothing more than the apprehension of an imagined similitude in normally unconnected things.)

Why then, I pondered—when the line of verse contradicted everything meteorology taught—did I like it? Perhaps it was the personification, the line's mythic properties. That, though, reeked of Plato and the romantics. Maybe, then, it was the illogicality, the irresponsibility of the thing. Was it possible that metaphor, and therefore poetry, were both insane? Maybe humans enjoyed dangling, for a moment, their feet in the pond of nonsense?

But that, too, was absurd. Art is everything to me, far more than nonsense. In fact, it is my reason for being.

And then I knew, it hit me. The reason I liked that damned line so much was because it WAS insane—irrational, and unscientific. In other words, it was pleasurable because it existed outside the known and knowable, because it contradicted what I *knew* and made me know, momentarily, the feeling of being free.

Free, free, free! "...the very word is like a bell, to toll me back... to my sole self!"

I understood, then, what my metaphor-rich world: Pond, and rose, and rhododendron, hawk, and serpent meant. Given the will and opportunity ("world enough and time"), I was free to see with unencumbered eyes the world I choose to see. My pen ran wild, and what I wrote—a mini-course in metaphor—follows:

> Originating new metaphors reminds us of our childhood, our Eden innocence, when metaphor-making was our most satisfying activity, when the world was a treasure-trove of metaphors. This explains the romantic emphasis on the child's eye and "wise passiveness." The child's eye had not yet been programmed to see the world from an adult perspective.
>
> The fact is that nature, as substance, is our original and therefore most common source

of metaphor. Nature redefined is substance undefiled.

The romantics' conclusion that nature was a repository of love-instigated sensations, that it "never did betray the heart that loved her," was based on the self-serving desire for absolute truth, a truth that inevitably leads to paganism. Freedom is forever threatened by security.

The fact is, no metaphor (poetic or scientific) is right or wrong. The words *efficient* or *inefficient*, *open-ended* or *boxed* are, for me, more accurate characterizations.

Art originates, not from Keats' version of truth or beauty, then, but from the inherent drive to create metaphors, to find metaphors that "work." (Work, in this sense, means safe arrival at survival.)

Metaphorical substance, the nonphysical stuff that's made from substance, is another name for art.

The fact that substance has no meaning until it has been "metaphorized" does not mean that substance does not exist. We were substance before we were anything.

We are free to "metaphorize" substance in any way we choose, but substance—except in cases of alchemy and scientific experiments—does not change to suit our metaphors.

Art is non-trapping metaphor, and being free to "metaphorize" substance as we please is the highest form of pleasure.

Freedom may be defined as the right to control the substance of substance—metaphor—in any way we choose.

Outside my study window now it's February. Snow blankets everything. The brambles and briers that threaten to choke my one apple tree are sere and stretch like stenciled squares for tic-tac-toe athwart a gray and wintry sunset.

To my left and up the mountain, Highway 276 wriggles its tortuous way toward Rich Mountain and a cabin surrounded by a pond frozen and fraught with snow. Nothing is reflected in that pond. The hawk, if wise, has flown away, and the serpent sleeps, well-fed and wise, beneath a certain slab of concrete. The roses, wasps, and rhododendron await the warmth of spring, and I do, too.

The world is rich with metaphors, and I have found my work.

A Contrarian View of Metaphor

A contrarian is an individual so dissatisfied with his current reality that he creates another more suited to his liking. I confess that in more recent writing, I have tended to omit reference to the artificial division of metaphor into three types spelled out below. I remain convinced, however, that metaphor is at the root of everything known to man. The concept presented here relies heavily on the science behind quantum mechanics which, it is believed, provides support for the philosophy of metaphor upon which all of my writing is based.

My proposed version of reality is that all reality is derived from metaphor—be it physical, as represented in the material world, or ideational, as in the form of mental constructs.

Anything capable of being held in the mind—be it in the mind that is nature or in the mind of humans—is a metaphor, and all metaphors are based on survival drive, the urge to discover and merge with affinities—to recreate themselves and thereby assure survival. Thus a negative particle seeks its sister; a positive electron seeks a negative, a cell divides into another cell, genes absorb traits from both parents to build a composite, and so it goes—on and on, hopefully forever or until that certain time when expansion drives all galaxies into oblivion.

The thing that makes a metaphor work is comparison, and it matters not a whit whether the comparisons are positive or negative, attractive or repulsive, asexual or sexual. Metaphors rely on discovered affinities, be they negative or positive—be they likenesses or differences. A negatively charged electron is attracted to a positive electron, not to a negative one. And, reverting to syntax, an active verb "recognizes" and seeks out its object in some form of noun.

Examples of metaphors in nature are limitless as stars, but it is metaphor as used in literature—specifically in my novel, **White in the Moon,** that is of primary interest here. Every letter in every word represents a sound, every word is a metaphor created from the assembly of letters—though what it is that's being compared may be long forgotten—and every sentence is metaphor with words ordered and structured by the grammarian's version of survival drive, syntax.

Defined as a literary device, metaphor is said to infer that one thing is another, and, interestingly, bits of matter (elementary particles) say the same. But, in the way of illustration, let us turn to Noyes' construction in his famous litany to a highwayman. The poem is rife with metaphors (as it is with rhymes and rhythm), but the one selected for discussion here goes as follows: "The road was a ribbon of moonlight…."

Now everyone recognizes that the road is not literally a ribbon and that no ribbon can actually be made of moonlight. Wherefore, then, the feeling we get of pleasure, of satisfaction, of completeness? The metaphor captures something that rings "true" in the mind, in the picture it conveys. This "truth" is conveyed by means of comparison, and it doesn't even matter if the metaphor is true or false, only if it is effective. The very concepts being argued for here, it should be pointed out, are themselves metaphors.

Metaphor is always "layered" in this fashion—the road, a literal thing that furthers commerce and trysting, is compared to a ribbon, a slightly less literal thing with connotations of decoration and seduction, that is saturated in a bath of moonlight—the essence of romance and trysting-times, par excellence. Lurking disguised and unnoticed at the root of the romantic metaphor is coition and the act ultimately responsible for human survival.

In the interests of definition, I propose the existence of three kinds of metaphor, one reflexive, one hylozoic, and the other synthetic.

The first type, reflexive, I see as demonstrated by automatic reactions, by responses like flinching at the approach of a projectile or a swinging bat. It is ingrained in the system and requires no conscious ideation. A crude mechanism, it—like all metaphors—is dedicated to survival, but in this case strictly to the survival of the genome. Although other more complex versions have evolved from it, its influence is still apparent in primitive responses (for instance) to skin color, sexual identities, and physical violence. An unthinking reliance on these kind of metaphors is the source of evil on the planet.

The second type metaphor, hylozoic, is dedicated to the manipulation of materials to facilitate physical survival. It is represented in the designing of tools and implements and extends all the way to swinging bridges and sky scrapers. It is a metaphorical derivative (evolution) of the first, but its realm of issue is survival of the physical self through the conscious creation of objects that make survival easier. Charging people for our expertise is, itself, a means to physical survival, but when the ego gets involved, hylozoic metaphors tend to shade into synthetic ones.

The third type of metaphor, synthetic, represents a significant advance over the other two in that the metaphorical slots occupied by physical constructs are here replaced by ideational concepts. It is through this development of metaphor that the issue of survival of the psychological self—a nonphysical construct (a metaphor!) designed to give humans the illusion of control in the realm of ego—has come to dominate modern civilization, including religion, the arts, and textbooks.

Growing out of this evolution was human consciousness and the knowledge that death, the antithesis to survival, is our ultimate destiny. This knowledge has led to many artifices of self-survival, ranging from rationalization, to mind-blank, from cryogenics to dreamed-up heavenly refuges.

Synthetic metaphors include the arts, the social sciences, and philosophy, including religions. It is a transmutation easily understood, given the metaphorical nature of metaphor, but it is not one easily undertaken, given the involvement of ego. Feuds start here, departmental rivalries fester, and wars are undertaken—all in the interest of ego preservation. It is also the realm of Rembrandt and Beethoven, Shakespeare, and the King James version of the Bible.

Now, mind you, there is much more to this business of metaphor than prettification. At the risk of repetition, let it be said again: The concept of survival is itself metaphor—in my mind, the first metaphor. One atom (molecule, particle, what not) discovers affinity in another and WHAM-MO! we have a marriage (and pregnancy).

That blending, that becoming as one, is "recognized" as a comparison found and completed, a eureka moment recognized in the "brain" as survival accomplished. Thus began the Linking-Log construction that is nature. I call it metaphor by extension. The same metaphor is involved in "me hungry now; me eat."

This brings me to another characteristic of metaphor: No metaphor is right or wrong, just efficient or not. Noyes' metaphor is efficient because it is effective—it compares two objects not conventionally seen as similar and makes them seem the same. This moment of affirmation is perceived in the mind as pleasing, as "true" and, by extension, as conducive to survival.

The connection Mestral found between cockle burrs and Velcro, Blake's perception of beauty in the rose, Wright's architectural dream of the Kaufman House—all are the same sorts of thing, as was the discovery of penicillin, the polio vaccine, and the Wright brothers' accomplishment of flight. Nothing known or yet to be discovered exists but through the magic of metaphor.

If it is true that the only freedom possible is mental (and I believe that to be the case), then mankind must perfect the art of the conscious metaphor. My novel, **White In The Moon,** aims to be that kind of thing.

Like those nesting Russian dolls, metaphors have metaphors built inside of metaphors, and the more complex the metaphor the more layers it will have. **White** In **The Moon** aims to be a many-layered, conscious metaphor.

For instance, the title is taken from a line in a poem by A. E. Housman that reads: "White in the moon the long road lies/That leads me from my love." I would like the reader to see the "long road" as my life and the "love" as my search for truth. The line is itself metaphor, and the title also has textual relevance, another metaphorical application. My son's cover-painting portrays a moon reflected in water, yet another metaphor.

As each character in the novel is a metaphor consciously created to achieve an artistic function, so do the characters live their lives on the basis of their metaphors—reflexive, hylozoic, and synthetic. In the same way, the consequences of their metaphors speak to the author's underlying theme(s), so that metaphor becomes a metaphor of metaphor, so on and so on, *ad infinitum.*

Furthermore, as the characters use conscious metaphors, actually going so far as to define them, the reader is expected to expand their meaning beyond what even their speakers are aware of.

The novel seeks to illustrate metaphor by its use of metaphor— thus the inclusion of poems, a play, a diary, and epistolary letters, each with metaphorical meanings of their own but with implications, also, for the underlying theme of the novel. The description of paintings and music is an attempt to incorporate other types of metaphor as well, as is the use of allusions, literary tropes, and other devices. The novel itself, the reader is reminded, is a metaphor.

Is believe the novel illustrates, as well, the function of survival in metaphor. The characters live their lives driven by survival metaphors, reflexive, hylozoic, and synthetic. Mossy Pond, its denizens and neighbors, is a metaphor of one expression of survival drive, as are the many sexual motifs and the exploration of the uses and consequences of racism. And, needless to say, the author himself hopes to survive his demise by the contributions the work makes to human understanding and individual self-actualization.

All the world is metaphor, and the end of metaphor (made responsibly) is life well-lived.

A Biographical Memoir
of Metaphor

The following is an autobiographical essay based around the conceit that, like everything else in the world, memories are metaphors—a truism if you accept my premise of comparison (the process of metaphor) being at the root of all formations— mineral, biological, or ideational. My memories—calcified formations recorded physically (but not ineffably) in the brain— served as grounding for the ideas spun out by the reflexive process of comparison, ideas made synthetic (i.e., ideational) or hylozoic by conscious synthetic metaphor.

The autobiography is an expurgated one, hinting broadly at psychological problems, but eliding all references to the effects of whippings by an insecure parent brutalized by hypercritical sisters-in-law, to say nothing of my excessively puritanical upbringing where sin, hellfire, and eternal damnation were ever-present maledictions, and where even a passing reference to sex was frowned upon and darkly forbidden.

This said, this memoir of my first twenty-one years is—to the best of my ability—an honest one and an accurate depiction of my early years and the burgeoning concept of metaphor.

My name is Eston Eugene Roberts and I am a metaphor—as are you and everything existing on this planet and in our universe. My physical existence began on or around the twelfth day of the fourth month in the year 1931, when a spurt of ejaculated sperm from the metaphor called Carl Daniel Roberts encountered a receptive ovum in the belly of another metaphor, one of opposite sex, called Arthurlene Sutton Roberts.

I remember nothing of this encounter, as I remember nothing of my metaphorical progenitor who—for reasons unknown to me—removed himself, early in my fourth year, from the immediate presences of my sister, my mother, and me. In pursuit of that metaphor called happiness, and doubtlessly propelled by that most immediate of metaphors—physical survival—my mother met and married James Charlie West—a metaphor encrusted by the preternatural consequences of personal and familial survival earned at any cost—including an education ending in the sixth grade.

Not wishing to get lost in jungles of hypothesis, I propose to continue this memoir of Eston Eugene Roberts (known in South Georgia as Bobby) by dwelling on those memories (also metaphors) actually existing in that human library that is my brain—itself a metaphor created in the interest of physical survival, not of me but of what I represent: the survival of biological matter.

The first memory of which I am aware occurred in my fourth year after my mother, sister, and I moved into the home of Gary Phillips, my mother's uncle—a man I remember only from pictures—in Damascus, GA.

Prefatory to this memory moment—a metaphor, mind you—someone had delivered a load of unstacked stovewood and deposited it in the yard on the north side of the house surrounded on two sides by porch. There was (what from the perspective of a four-year-old) a tall oak tree on the northeast side of the fenced-in yard stretching its bole and branches skyward. I recall vividly deciding to stack the wood against the tree in such a fashion as to enable me to climb to the sky. The metaphor ends with the thought, but I like to think its influence has guided my life.

After this earliest of memories (chronologies get mixed and old photographs and family mythologies entangle), the actuality of memories become suspect. Even so, my next earliest memory is of my stepfather—young, recently married, and deeply in love— strong is his expectations of making a life not based on farming—lifting me up to the rafters in our bedroom and allowing me to drop unimpeded onto the bed in our rented shanty in Pinetops, GA. As it registers in my mind today, this experience was the very apogee of exhilaration.

There are other, flash-bulb-like memories of those times in Pinetops, GA., and later in Boms, FL., where my stepfather ran a sparsely stocked country store and my mother, in addition to house-wifely activities, raised White Leghorn chickens; but my next certifiable memories are school-related, though they are few and widely dispersed. I do not remember, for instance, any events in my first or second years in school. I do not remember learning to read—though there was a family myth that I taught myself that skill—but that escapist world of reading was always my preferred realm of existence.

At some point in time, my step-father's dream of escaping the harsh world of subsistence living faltered, and we moved back in with his parents in their large log home built from logs harvested from still-virgin forests cleared by ancestors named Hilburn. My family was assigned the large, southernmost room—a room occupied, still, by an aged pump organ and dark, brooding photographs of dark, brooding people that, in retrospect, might've been purloined from the Earnshaw home place in **Wuthering Heights**.

My first school-related memory is of me in a line of marching children—Bethany Elementery was divided into two sections, one the main brick structure, and the other wooden adjuncts added as the student body increased in numbers—and I remember a teacher guiding her caravan of students in the opposite direction from the lunchroom calling out to our teacher: "Oh, I see you have a cowboy in your class!"

I distinctly remember exulting in that glow of recognition, even though my mother had long before decreed that I could no longer wear the filthy outfit to school. (The outfit, a gift of a favorite aunt in Jacksonville, FL., had gotten wrinkled, dingy, and soiled to the point of rottenness.) But I, in my Ariesean stubbornness, had refused to acquiesce and, instead, took my cowboy outfit down to the bus stop and hid it in an obliging grove of gallberry bushes.

Each morning I would remove my school clothes, hide them in the bushes, and replace them with my transformational fringed shirt, leather vest, leggings, and high-heeled boots— the boots long outgrown and requiring the painful bending of toes to accommodate their insertion.

My next school memory, and it is still sequential, occurred in the fourth or fifth grade. I know this because by this time I and my peers were ensconced in a classroom in the original structure. Again, I recall nothing about reading or arithmetic, but I recall distinctly my raising my hand excitedly and volunteering the information that my grandfather had once operated a moonshine still on a raft in Mossy Pond. I recall, also, being disappointed when the teacher tactfully changed the discussion to another subject.

In the fifth grade I published my first poem, "My Conscience," in the Miller County weekly newspaper. I remember exulting in my mind, "Move over Shakespeare!" I was all of nine years old and had a lot to learn! Until the day she died my mother opined, "It was the best poem you ever wrote."

I was in the seventh grade when my next recalled memory occurred. One of our fellow students—a Huck-Finn genotype, prone to tardiness, playing the truant, and being, most generally, a thorn in the side of all activities imbued with authority—had successfully infuriated Mrs. Taylor, a buxom woman with an appropriately majestic bosom, to the point where she was emphatically telling him to report, at once, to the principal's office.

This young man, this outlaw secretly admired by us all—knowing too well the consequences accompanying such a visit—refused to budge and, instead, picked up the softball bat positioned inside the door jamb, and threatened to "brain" Mrs. Taylor. As it turned out, that softball bat belonged to me, and for a week or so I lived in reflected glory, admired by my classmates for making possible their involvement in an epic episode of powerful import. We had all witnessed it first-hand—the defiance of unquestioned authority and unmitigated power!

My next school memory—and the reader is reminded that memories are metaphors implanted by calcium in brain cells—is set in the same classroom in the purview of that previously mentioned Amazonian, Mrs. Taylor. All my years in Georgia I had lived surrounded on two sides by swamps and ponds; consequently, I was familiar with and foolishly unafraid of all manners of reptile.

It was, then, no a matter of great consequence when I discovered, during recess, a green grass snake wrapped around the limbs of a persimmon tree on the edge of the school yard. It was in an almost innocent act of mischief that I took the snake back with me to the classroom and placed it in the top drawer of Mrs. Taylor's desk.

As the day wore down, all of us watched in great anticipation as our teacher walked back and forth in the classroom, approaching the desk but never opening the drawer. It was nearing the three o' clock hour when she finally opened the drawer. By then, the sequestered reptile was feeling pent, and it was not a great surprise that it leapt out and landed directly onto Mrs. Taylor's ample bosom. She screamed a surprisingly shrill scream and scrambled rapidly to the back of the classroom. (Some pundits present avowed [doubtlessly in a less-grown vocabulary] that never in their lives had they seen three-hundred pounds of woman move with such alacrity!)

When decorum was eventually restored, Mrs. Taylor went around the room, pointing a pudgy, angry forefinger in every young man's face, seeking unsuccessfully the villainous culprit. Interestingly, she never got around to accosting me, I being the epitome of the well-behaved, dedicated student.

Once again, and for an admittedly brief period of time, I waxed glorious in the glow of an unearned fame.

There are other flash-bulb-type memories, but the next most salient ones occurred in the eighth grade. For reasons of my having outgrown Bethany Elementary, I was transferred to Elmodel High just north of Newton, Georgia. It was a twenty-mile trek by bus, necessitating that I be at the bus stop before daybreak.

At Bethany Elementary everybody had known me, my parents, and knew of the two-room shanty we lived in. But at Elmodel, nobody knew me from Adam. Consequently, I feigned (in my mind) richness, keeping coins—oftentimes at the expense of lunch—in my right-hand pocket, coins which I jingled constantly. (To this day, I find myself reflexively continuing the same activity.) But the purpose, in my mind, was to keep my classmates from imagining the pitiable level of poverty that was my lot.

Whatever the reasons, my memories of Elmodel are pleasant ones. There was the time when—shutting my eyes and swinging as hard as I could—I connected bat with baseball and sent it rolling far into the shrubbery below the classroom windows. It was (according to the basketball coach) the farthest any one had ever hit a ball before!

(I also fashioned, from rust-encumbered files brought from home, fragile knives on the school shop's emery wheel—knives that gleamed like silver in sunlight and crumbled like toast when dropped!)

And then there was this young and attractive History teacher, probably fresh out of college, who announced to the class that I was the smartest boy in school—a ploy I now recognize as a psychological one. On one occasion she placed the history test on my desk—complete with answers—and avowed as she left the room that she knew I would never look at them. I would've bearded any beast that ventured near them!

While at Elmodel I read every book of fiction in the limited library and sold book reports for 25 cents apiece. (Billy Vines still owes me ninety cents!) In those days, all males took FFA (Future Farmers of America) classes, and I still remember the words written on the blackboard by the Elmodel ag teacher: ***Hemorrhagic Septicemia, Pasteurilla Pseudo Bacterium Diphtherium.*** I took great delight in saying them as one word. The fourth word I remember pronouncing as *pee-sudo.*

There was a veteran of the Second World War enrolled in our class—not, by any means the sharpest tool in the drawer!—and he delighted in demonstrating how he would smoke on sentry duty and invert the lighted cigarette into his mouth when accosted by a superior. He also recounted to trembling young ears his stories of sexual conquests in Germany, buried up to his neck in beachfront waters.

After one year at Elmodel, my parents transferred my sister and me to Damascus High, a school nearer home but in a different county. (We had to walk to the county line to catch the bus.) At Damascus High, everybody knew us, so my pretension of being rich was no longer practical, and my memories from there, possibly not coincidentally, are unhappy ones. It was there in my senior year, though, that the school principal took an interest in me and determined that I should go to college.

I had never even entertained the possibility of college and, as a result, had taken no college preparatory classes. This wonderful lady (Mrs. Alexander) tutored me in civics and algebra, and doctored my transcript so that I could be admitted to Berry College, a self-help institution north (barely) of Rome, Georgia.

I was seventeen years of age when I arrived—working that first summer on the garden crew at 27 cents an hour—and the succeeding fall semester, the stress condition that had so complicated my elementary years returned with a vengeance.

I remember very little of that year—all first-year males being domiciled at the Boys' high school some distance away from the main campus. I do recall that I had five roommates and our arm-wrestling for the top bunks, I coming out the winner of one of them. I recall the jock itch that assailed us all and the application of fiery salicylic acid—Marion Sanders fanning his nether regions vigorously with his bath towel. The only classes I remember with any detail was the summer school history course under Mr. Rooks at the main campus, my freshman Botany class under Miss Clendinen, and English classes where I was once praised (and chastised) for my use of *myriad*.

It was in this class that the teacher required us to write a short story. Short stories spilled out of me like water from a freshet, and I sold a great many of them, later on, for five dollars each. I recall, during my senior year, a freshman coming to me and asking for a story. I told him the only one I had left I had submitted a synopsis of to the teacher, though I'd turned in another story. He was willing to take the risk and, as I learned later, with dire consequences. He failed the course!

My sophomore year we all moved to the main campus, and those first two semesters are almost a total blank. I am now convinced, looking back on it, that I underwent, during that year, some sort of psychological shutdown. I have flash-bulb-style memories of a sidewalk and trees on the way to a classroom, a vaguely-remembered journalism class taught by Dean Cook, for which I wrote an essay on Ernie Pyle, and a roommate from North Georgia with protruding front teeth named Willie Skinner. He majored in Accounting. That year I also captured, and made a pet of, a chipmunk—a development I regularly wrote about in my journal.

I worked in succeeding semesters on the campus crew (mowing grass and collecting trash) and in the winter and spring on the housekeeping crew, sweeping and mopping floors. I was active in the Religious Education Club, was elected president, and considered myself in training to be an evangelist—realizing, even then, that conventional religion was not for me.

At the end of my sophomore year—subject to considerable parental pressure—I withdrew from school and tried to join the Navy. Completing enlistment was stymied by my not having brought my birth certificate, and, not being in a rush, I delayed my return. In the meantime, the recruiting officer sent for my college transcript, and to my great surprise, and my mother's fierce disappointment, a red Studebaker, driven by the college chaplain, showed up at our door. It was a three-hundred-mile trip, and how he found me I will never know!

After an hour's teary-eyed discussion under a towering red cypress near the highway, Dr. R. C. Gresham gave me twenty dollars and told me to get back to college where a job would be waiting for me. Any necessary expenses, he said, would be covered by him. My mother hated him to her dying day, saying, "He stole my boy."

In many respects she was right, because I went back to school with a determined interest in philosophy. I remember distinctly, when in my junior year, stumbling onto the works of Thomas Paine, and, under the force of his logic and disrespect for the Bible, the foundations of my fundamental Christian teachings crumbling like chaff. Driven, doubtlessly, by the adolescent aversion to dependency, I rewarded the chaplain's generosity by professing atheism and announcing it to the alumni bulletin where, naturally enough, it was brought to his attention.

For my senior year, I borrowed money from a well-to-do relative and accepted no further assistance from Dr. Gresham. Upon receiving my first paycheck in the Marine Corps, I wrote him, asking him to let me know what I owed so that I could begin paying him back. His response: "I won't accept any money. Just do the same thing for some other deserving person."

The wily old fox. I've been paying him back ever since!

It was during my senior year that I experienced the world-altering discovery of my life. I remember it well. I was sitting in the photography lab at Berry College, reading an article by Fred Hoyle—even then a famous cosmologist—in **Life Magazine**. It was about his theory of continuous creation, a concept he was later to renounce, whereby planets recreated themselves after destruction by an instilled drive in nature to accumulate dust and debris.

It was then that it occurred to me I could apply his theory of creation to formulating my own philosophy of life. Though I did not know it then—and it was forty years later when I ran into its scientific underpinning, quantum mechanics—that I had discovered metaphor, the instilled drive in nature to accumulate the dust and debris of human experience!

The rest, as they say, is history.

Rejoinder to Mumpower

*The following essay is an unpublished response to a letter (not reprinted here) to the editor of the **Asheville Citizen-Times** written by Carl Mumpower and is included here as commentary on how the subterranean (reflexive) tides of racism can subliminally ex-press themselves and as evidence of the worrisome fact that even intelligent individuals can be driven by the unexamined drive to survive to defend the indefensible. Mr. Mumpower is a practicing psychologist, has served on the Asheville (NC) City Council, was a past candidate for the N.C. House of Representatives, and is currently serving as Chairman of the Buncombe County Republican Party.*

Be ye not deceived. Carl Mumpower's "Guest Opinion" of 10/15/06 is a veiled attack on the black citizens of Asheville and beyond. In this reader's opinion, the problems and solutions he so glibly detail point to the very source of the problems he laments.

The careful reader will have detected—beneath the "thin veneer" of his protestations about "the immaturity of racism" and his baseball metaphor of "third-base" racial progress—a repellent usage of racist code-words and phrases suggesting that his professed tolerance is, in fact, smokescreen—benevolence cloaked in a sheepskin of racial prejudice.

Witness, for instance, such code-word references as "paralyzing attitudes of victimization," "political correctness," "indifference," "intimidation," and "pandering"; his employment of the words "ho" and "b---h," "bling," "rap," and "NBA;" and the catalog of "not O. K." behaviors—all portraying racist stereotypes. Finally, take note of his hate-filled malediction about "entrenched social predators milking government entitlements bought with the labor of others." These are not the words of a humanitarian, and his real target could not be clearer.

While it may seem, upon first reading, that Council member Mumpower talks a good game with his use of the words *culture*, *character*, and *choice*, a careful analysis of his vocabulary speaks to a reflexive current of bias, hate, and self-righteous anger.

And when viewed through the eyes of young blacks, the words *culture*, *character*, and *choice* are seen as little more than code-words for coercion—epithets chosen to support a view of reality that not only preserves the status quo, but that, not coincidentally, supports the right-wing conservative's view of reality.

A culture forced by laws and custom to conform to the predominant culture is a culture imprisoning as painfully as incarceration in actual prisons and, moreover, assures the consequences of socially mandated segregation: hopelessness, drug problems, high rates of school dropout, accidental pregnancies, dead-end employment, and joblessness.

If that same dominant culture defines character and choice—tolerating only behaviors that conform to its way of being—then the possibility for minority equality translates into another way of saying, "Be white like me or do not be at all."

If the reason for government is truly justice for all, then let us begin today to provide for the common welfare—to feed and house our hungry, and to truly educate our children. Let's clear our prisons of social scapegoats, outlaw demagoguery, declare warfare illegal, and assume responsibility for consciously and responsibly constructing self-images intolerant of subversive metaphors that lead us into know-it-all pontification of the sort demonstrated by Carl Mumpower.

Either we are more than our impulses, or we are nothing.

Conversation On A Certain Topic

The following essay is an outgrowth of a recent discussion with friends on the necessity for integrity in a world grown increasingly subjective. To that end, I resurrected an unfinished essay on an unexpected pregnancy and the subsequent abortion. After weeks of frustration and a nagging sense of dissatisfaction, however, I was awakened in the middle of the night with the conviction that I was addressing the wrong issue—that the real subject of my endeavors (and the cause for my angst) was the number of life events that had the effect of intervening between me and my search for a realized sense of self, events that waked in me consuming feelings of inferiority.

Abortion, I concluded, had been but one of several intervening impediments to self-realization, many of them (interestingly) involving sexual misadventures. Consequently, I decided to redirect my efforts to self-concept actualization and the role of integrity in it.

The above reference to sexual misadventures may merit further amplification. From the perspective of this essay (traumatic though they may have been), these may not have been coincidental interventions, given the fact of sex drive being an early expression of the drive to survive—the metaphor, in fact, behind the creation of all matter. There is, in other words, a natural rivalry between these forms of creation, the physical and the metaphorical, the procreative and the psychological.

This said—and in hopes of providing the reader insight and understanding—I propose, now, to present the philosophical underpinning for my continuing trek to self-actualization by detailing the thought processes I went through in reaching what I hope is a realized sense of self capable of living honorably in a highly subjective world. Reader patience and perseverance is advised.

The brain, I have come to see as a biological and chemical machine engineered early on to ensure and facilitate physical survival. Over eons of successful and abortive metaphorical experiments driven by survival drive, nature produced a facsimile of itself called self-concept, setting in place a contest for dominance that continues to this day.

Arrival at the point of self-concept (through the process Charles Darwin named evolution) made it possible for individuals to initiate conscious actions in interest of their personal survival—a far more efficient process than the built-in, reflexive one used by the original physical survival metaphor. As time passed, this transition (conscious decision-making) led, paradoxically, to creation of that metaphorical sense of self Freud named ego, a rival son (powered by survival drive!) to its parent.

Because this metaphorical creation—I prefer, for my purposes, the usage self-concept—retained its access to reflexive survival drive (the proclivity to respond automatically to perceived threats to physical survival), humans were able to invent evasive tactics such as rationalization, misrepresentation, and, yes, even reflexive self-deception—all in the interests of ego survival.

These tactics of self-deception, it should be noted, constitute a defensive way of protecting self-concept from its metaphorical counterpart in the real world, the fear of dying—its equivalence, in the case of self-concept, being the expression of self-doubt—and, despite the new-found capacity for consciousness, the easiest survival-path was, and remains, mind-blank—a refusal to confront and deal with psychological threats, unerased threats that fester and eat away at self-esteem.

And, while—thanks to the tactics of self-deception—it was now possible to lie to ourselves, the newfound agency of awareness made it impossible to do so without knowing it; and lying leads, inevitably, to the accumulation of self-doubts—the fulminating cause of our inability to act assertively in our own best interests. This leads, in turn, to the obviation of a confident sense of self—the extreme of which is insanity.

This remembrance of past imbroglios, ironically, gave humans the choice—as it turned out a very important one—of recognizing and resisting (if they chose) reflexive programming in all its many permutations, including—reference the burgeoning "Me Too!" movement—the drive for sex.

This discovery of self-monition made it possible to condition one's concept of self to consciously recognize (and abjure) metaphors driven by physical survival drive—reflexive metaphors being inimical to consciousness and, ultimately, to choice and the possibility for individual freedom.

It became possible, in other words, to take responsibility for one's own life, to recognize (and reject) thoughts and actions in interest of integrity metaphors provoked by physical survival drive—the basis, as proposed here, for integrity.

Self-concept, then, is viewed here as a self-created, evolving metaphor whose existence is owed (like matter) to the survival impulse. Created consciously, as a result of elected actions and ideas conditioned by the concept of integrity—the process of self-concept construction recommended here—the metaphor that is self-concept becomes the arbiter of both awareness (consciousness) and reality.

As it turns out, this arrival at self-concept assertiveness is not a matter of merely taking thought. Because reflexive metaphors originated in the world of matter, they are the model of metaphorical efficiency—the one-on-one affinity between elements making this so. Either particle constituents "match" or they don't; either they are compatible or they aren't. Either a metal is subject to magnetic attraction or it isn't; this berry is edible or it's poisonous. In the world of matter, subjectivity does not exist.

Unfortunately, this is not the case in the world of mind where metaphors are mental and where access is granted to all affinities—presumed or actual, even those containing logical incompatibilities—with the most powerful survival issue (physical or psychological) determining the particular concept selected for utilization and/or emphasis.

For instance, issues of belief, like truth and faith—powerful motivators in the survival of self—are thus subject to choice; and the reflexively created sense of self is naturally inclined to that expression of survival drive made easiest by instinct. In this instance, choices are often predetermined. As stated elsewhere: There are consequences to the casual use of metaphor.

I turn, now, to the implications and underlying applications of the philosophy of metaphor argued for here—my belief that unthinking susceptibility to subliminal survival drive is responsible for much of the evil on the planet.

In support of the premise about reflexive thinking I now turn to an analysis of a Rush Limbaugh statement (extracted with apologies for settling for a secondary source) from a quote by Leonard Pitts **Asheville Citizen-Times,** (4E, 9/17/2017). In the citation, there are diverse elements supporting the dubious proposition that liberal thinkers look favorably on hurricanes, a hypothesis that reeks of reflexive survival drive. Pitts writes (quoting Limbaugh):

> It is in the interest of the left to have destructive hurricanes... because then they can blame it [destruction] on climate change.... So the media benefits with the panic and increased eyeballs, *and* the retailers benefit from the panic with increased sales.

The assumption underlying the first sentence is that liberals take advantage of hurricanes—the more destructive the better—to support the unproven concept of climate change—an insidious invention (as perceived by Limbaugh and his disciples) of tax-hungry liberals meant to destroy capitalism—the perfect economic personification of the drive to survive.

Underlying Limbaugh's argument is the belief that negating the liberal apostasy would return us to a world and time where everything was "great" again, where "millions" of new jobs would be created, where a reduction in industry-sapping taxes would be accomplished, and the elimination of the public "dole" realized—all eventualities notable for their applicability to physical survival).

It's the replaying of the ongoing conflict between two forms of survival—physical survival versus self-concept survival, primitive pragmatism, (staying alive is the only thing that really matters)—versus that more modern way of thinking exemplified in conscious metaphor.

The second sentence in the Limbaugh citation assumes that media [Fox News excepted?] is liberal and that an increase in reader numbers profits liberal "eyeballs," by—it is assumed—selling and pedaling their invidious ideology of tax and spend.

This is followed by the assertion that retailers (also apparently liberal?) enjoy increased profits from the panic caused by the left's support of climate change—a fabricated threat (as he sees it) to the established order and an excuse for increased taxes—another perfidious threat to old-time survival, one promulgated (naturally) by liberals.

Again, it can be seen, Limbaugh's argument revolves around issues related to the physical survival imperative, with the point being made that liberals gain support for their heresies (gun control, abortion rights, taxes?) through emphasis on climate change, a stand-in, from Limbaugh's perspective, of change inspired by evil. It is hardly coincidental that evangelicals (by and large) ride his wagon—note the metaphor!

Driving the entire Limbaugh statement and powering its subliminal hostility is the force that is primal survival urge—the apparent antithetical force to progressive ideas. The "panic" allegedly devolving from liberal propaganda can be seen as a direct appeal by Limbaugh to primitive survival impulses and its entrenched abhorrence of the thought of dying. That the subliminal energy goes unrecognized by Limbaugh only confirms its existence.

Thus it may be said with confidence: Logically inconsistent ideas may contain elements that evoke the reflexive response, and strongly held ideas (in this case the primacy of physical survival) can find affinities where they do not exist.

Limbaugh's one-sided perspective bespeaks a psychology hooked on the need for certainty, a security, it will be argued, purchased at the cost of integrity.

The premise that instinctive forces underlie and promulgate Limbaugh's argument may account for its hostility and dearth of logical thinking, but it points, as well, to the possibility of a more tragic consequence. Allowing reflexive survival drive to do our thinking for us risks turning us into unthinking robots, willing victims of a failure to do the work necessary to enrichment of our humanness and advancement of the human race.

Unthinking adherents of the Limbaugh point of view risk a similar abeyance to hidden forces and a willful rejection of the human responsibility to do its own thinking—a decision made, as argued here, at the cost of self-empowerment, personal integrity, and, ultimately, the very possibility of mental freedom.

The "work"—the advancement of the human race—referred to above, the triumph, in other words, of a positive sense of self over reflexive survival drive—involves the conscious development of self-concept by doing those things necessary to feeling good about the metaphor that is our self-created selves.

This process is achieved by the individual's determined refusal to accede to the promptings of reflexive mental processes, processes leading to such predictive consequences as hegemony, religious bigotry, racial bias, blind patriotism, and the use of physical violence—symptoms, everyone, of an irresponsibly developed sense of self and witness, thereby, to the absence of integrity as defined herein.

It is through the conscious employment of integrity— recognizing and rejecting reflexive responses—that the concept of self can be self-constructed; and lying to oneself, (ignoring, for instance, established scientific fact in stubborn abeyance to reflexive concepts) is the acid that eats at the roots of a positive self-image, the metaphor (as it turns out) that is the ultimate arbiter of reality and determiner of the tracks we leave on the face of history.

The concept of integrity argued for here—that humans cannot lie to themselves in the interest of easy survival and prosper psychologically—is owed to my belief that the knowledge of death, and the fear of it, pervades human consciousness and (as the stimulus behind survival drive) incentivates reflexive thinking.

It is, I believe, the responsibility of every human to live honorably with mortality and to resist, as the death it is, the tendency to fabricate memes like heaven or reincarnation to hide the fear of dying, actions that affirm subservience to reflexive survival drive and constitute, as well, a fatal violation of the sense of an earned integrity.

The same can be said of those unearned feelings of worth gained from conforming to the tenets of a faith-based dream of eternal life. While practicing works of faith can redound to the benefit of humanity, believing that such endeavors lead to heavenly rewards reeks of survival instinct and the onus of escaping death—another self-serving hypocrisy that undermines self-concept.

Supportive expressions of primitive survival drive—this time sublimated into the security of certainty—may be found in the reflexive acceptance of the credo of the National Rifle Association and by buying unthinkingly into the view of abortion fostered by evangelicals.

Objections to gun-control—despite professed support for legal restraints on the mentally ill—itself an expression of reflexive metaphor's antipathy to difference—and the movement's grudging approval of background checks—are grounded in the drive for physical survival and can be traced to primitive instincts once purposed for protecting territory (reference immigration), for staying alive, and for finding food—purposes rendered irrelevant by laws and technology in modern times and evidence, besides, of continued utilization of primitive instincts.

The repeated (and selective) invocation of the constitutional right to bear arms—Where, one is compelled to ask, is comparable emphasis on "all men are created equal..."?—is supportive, also, of the role played by the urge to survive physically and is reminiscent, as well, of sentiments found in evangelicals' insistence on the Bible being the inviolate word of God.

The need for absolutes—for perfect truths— is an enduring characteristic of reflexive thinking and can be seen as an expression of feelings of insecurity induced by the fear of dying. Raising counter issues of gun powder and blunderbusses, questioning (God forbid!) the infallibility of a document written by citizens of the eighteenth century, while reasonable and logical, face automatic rejection in the face of hardened beliefs grounded in the need for the security of certainty.

The version of integrity fostered here—being honest with one's self—cannot abide the creation of metaphors based on denial and a sublimated fear of dying.

Similar frozen absolutes are found in many discussions of abortion. When looked at objectively, from the viewpoint of nature, a pregnancy is a technological response to a technological action. Sperm meets egg propitiously, and pregnancy occurs. Except in case of physiological defects, pregnancies proceed according to the physical laws of physical survival, miscarriages (like abortions) having no meanings other than the ones we assign to them. Survival is nature's business, its only business.

This said, the most pervasive absolute, with respect to abortion and, in the mind of evangelicals, is the belief that human life is sacred—a metaphor pregnant(!) with physical survival drive.

Aside from the presumptive arrogance implicit in such an assumption, sheer honesty requires that we recognize the profligacy with which fertilizable eggs are strewn across the natural landscape—the more specimens born, the greater the odds of survival—a pragmatism that underlies the primacy nature assigns physical survival.

Moreover, the notion of sacredness obviously derives from belief in the presumed existence of an all-wise deity who, in addition to having created all material forms—including the very stars above us and the planet on which we reside, and who created us in His own image, besides—is in charge of everything. To "kill" a baby, from this perspective, is tantamount to killing God and—by extension—to affirming the impossibility of life after death. Talk about survival metaphors? This is the granddaddy of them all!

Furthermore, advancing the paroxysms of guilt experienced by women undergoing abortion procedure as evidence of divine opposition speaks directly to the success of religious indoctrination, the desire to avoid dying, and, not coincidentally, demonstrates the lack of nuance in the vocabulary of the primitive drive to survive. Its words are limited to *conducive or aversive,* and pain (in the converted) is rendered *guilt.*

Additionally, integrity compels us to recognize that reflexive survival practices (nothing sacred here!) lead to over-population, world-wide hunger—and, to say nothing of species extinction—to wars and pestilence (again, nothing sacred here!)

It must be obvious to even the most biased of readers that birth control (of whatever type) and the elimination of unwanted pregnancies are outgrowths of conscious thinking, not reflexive metaphors! And furthermore, as stated, abortion has no meaning save the ones we assign it, and the hysterical objection to it is persuasive evidence of the propulsive power of the reflexive drive to survive.

Finally, it is important to stress that practicing integrity involves a great deal more than recognizing and rejecting metaphors germinated by primitive survival drive. In fact, recognition of the generative force of primitive survival drive is but the first step on the path to self-generated metaphors. The practice of integrity requires the deliberate action of substituting self-enhancing thoughts and actions for those emotional and reflexive responses suggested by the primitive stimulus.

It is, of course, those actions taken in the real world—on the basis of conscious thought—that ground our metaphors, that give them actuality in the world and in the mind. As said in the Bible: "Faith without works is dead." It is to that end that I engage in strenuous physical activity three times a week. Like the determination not to lie to one's self, it is a conscious investment in self-concept—in feeling good about myself in body and mind.

One final instance supportive of reflexive response may be seen in the impulse to racism—an instinctive reaction to the threat of difference. It is a reaction entirely aversive to the practice of integrity proposed here. Not only is the response a reflexive one, it has the effect of denying dignity (the right of unconditioned acceptance) to another human being on grounds based on reflex, not election.

(Anecdotal experiences about racial encounters only confirm primitive stimulus since they are inevitably summoned in support of prejudice.)

The moment, then, when reaction to a racial stimulus is recognized, the individual dedicated to the version of integrity promoted here will consciously reject the metaphor of racism and substitute for it the idea of tolerance (and specific actions) based on principle. The action of a friendly handshake, or sincere greeting—to say nothing of open resistance to the practice—supports and confirms investment in self-concept enhancement.

If the version of integrity proposed here, if you entertain thoughts of individual freedom and the empowerment that comes from an actualized self-concept, then the following conscious actions may appeal to you:

> Befriend the friendless;
> Feed the hungry;
> Speak truth to power;
> And this above all: "....to thine own self be true,

And it must follow, as the night the day,
Thou cans't not then be false to any man."

—Wm. Shakespeare

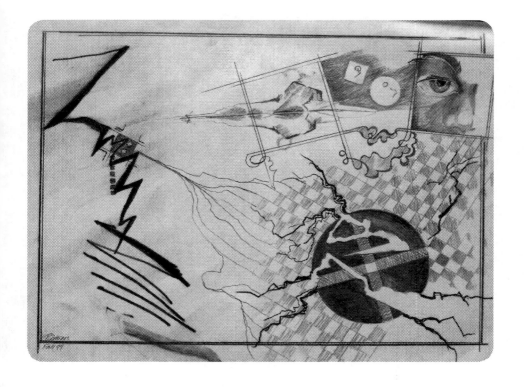

Everything Is Metaphor

The following essay was written for presentation to Lagniappe, a men's group that meets weekly in Brevard, N.C., to discuss and ruminate on a variety of topics ranging from the philosophical to the mundane, from the political to the scatological. The essay was presented, jokingly, as an attempt to "elevate" the general level of conversation.

> In the beginning God created the heaven and the earth. And the earth was without form, and void; and darkness was upon the face of the deep. And the spirit of God moved on the face of the waters.
>
> **Genesis**, KJV, I, 1-3

Let us begin by recognizing that the typical definition of metaphor as a figure of speech that says one thing is another is seriously flawed. Far from being a figure of speech, metaphor is the very method by which existence is formed. It was born in that moment when one cosmic particle (virtual rather than actual?) collided in space and discovered affinity—this first marriage, the source of pleasure, and the basis of that drive to consummate, I call survival drive.

The conventional definition of metaphor is further flawed by its assertion that one thing is another. Metaphor is recognition of affinity, of compatibility found in another object. This recognition makes possible that linking of object (or idea) into a construction driven to seek out new and unthought-of connections, the very method of survival in the natural world. Far from saying one thing is another, the word *metaphor* (itself a metaphor) is descriptive of an ingrained, ongoing survival process—the creation of another related (albeit distinct and separate) object, in nature or in the mind.

In nature, metaphors are material conglomerates—things like trees, birds, planets. In literature, we see them as individual figures, as in "The road was a ribbon of moonlight...," when, in fact, they are more likely to manifest themselves in constructions like essays, poems, and novels. The quote from **Genesis**, above, is an instance of this. To the extent that the book of **Genesis** is a coherent whole, it is also a metaphor.

This said, for purposes of discussion, I have divided metaphor into three types—all three evolutionary products of the forementioned survival drive—they are reflexive, hylozoic, and synthetic.

I see reflexive metaphors as instinctive and as representing that earliest, most primitive expression of survival drive. They are dedicated to survival of the physical self and are represented in the sunflower's tracking of the sun, the blinking of an eye to avoid a tree limb, and the mother bear's impulse to protect her young. Like all metaphors, reflexive metaphors are subject to mutative expression, and over centuries of evolution they have been adapted to the synthetic (see below) metaphors of language and psychology.

Hylozoic metaphors are one step removed from the reflexive and represent an evolution of the physical survival impulse applied to the invention of tools—the use of a twig, for instance, by a chimpanzee in extracting a termite from its hill. The beaver employs it in the creation of dams, the spider in her creation of intricate webs, and humans in the construction of roads, bridges, and tractors. Like all metaphors, they facilitate survival—physical and (when synthetic) psychological.

Synthetic metaphors are products of the survival impulse applied to that evolving idea of self. Their concern is exclusively psychological—that is, they are concerned with survival of self and are the most modern expression of the survival motive. In humans, they are represented in language, the arts, sciences, history, religions, and in the various forms of mental illnesses. Like all metaphors, they are subject to "infiltration" by their predecessors.

This susceptibility to infiltration means that there is no such thing as an uncontaminated metaphor, reserved as pure unto itself. Any metaphor is subject to the influence of the other two types, giving it the capacity to shade into the other, and in doing so reduce (or eliminate) the likelihood of a pure metaphor ever existing. That does not mean—and this is important— that we are not capable of identifying the dominant survival force behind a metaphor and consciously choosing whether or not to be influenced by it.

The self-concept, itself subject to unconscious metaphoric "bleeding," is seen as a synthetic metaphor, primarily conscious, and employable as the tool of discernment. This means we can analyze our metaphors, identify their dominant energy, refuse to allow them control over our behavior, and assume responsibility—accept blame or celebrate results—for their influence on our phenomenal selves.

By taking thought, we can take control of the human souls we choose to be, being free, thereby, in the only sense that is really possible.

I cannot end this piece without addressing the implications of this philosophy to some selected aspects of modern living.

1. *(Commentary: While there is nothing inherently evil in the impulse to survive, be it physically or psychologically, there are consequences to allowing reflexive metaphors to dominate our thinking—among them, irresponsible behaviors, unpremeditated anger, and physical violence. We can be motivated to scrounge, to horde, to ogle women—all reflexively, without conscious choice. Moreover, reflexive metaphors have a way of encouraging easy answers, superstitious responses, and instinctive prejudices. It behooves us, as humans dedicated to being the best human we can be, to avoid that approach to survival that is instinctive, unthinking, and irresponsible.)*

2. Politics and Government: The reflexive impulse to survive, all too often expressed in the search for power, is a manifestation of the impulse to physical survival applied to money and to ego. While the metaphorical structure that is government seeks to structure our lives in the interest of preventing anarchy—assuring the continuation of necessary services, and providing protection from potential attackers—the underlying imperative of physical survival drive is still evident. Problems like graft and embezzlement occur when the reflexive impulse to survive overrides synthetic ones, as in the willed resolve to do good.

3. The predominant metaphorical force behind the current Republican nominee for the presidency, Donald J. Trump, is clearly reflexive. He talks about health care, relief from excessive taxation, and support for equal rights for women, at the same time, mouthing metaphors about organ size, menstrual cycles, disabilities, and physical unattractiveness—all addressing issues of fundamental bodily functions and clearly reflexively driven. His exhortations to the use of military might are also illustrative, as is his continual reference to building a wall to reflexive impulse. His appeal is to those individuals unfortunately characterized as "deplorables," persons whose lives are geared primarily by the use of unexamined, reflexive metaphor.

People committed to recognizing and taking responsibility for the impulses governing their metaphors could never vote for him.

4. Religion: Every established religion, with the possible exception of Buddhism, is traceable to the drive to survive the fact of death, death being the antithesis of survival and a powerful agent in the lives of humans—cursed as we are by the twin facts of history and memory. Like all metaphors (and again) all metaphors are survival-based, religious metaphors may be predominately empowered by the reflexive survival impulse.

   This is evident in those fundamental doctrines where sermons deal fervently with lurid depictions of the horrors of hell, the evils (and bloodiness) of abortion, the consequences of demon rum, and the threats of an omnipresent devil. It is no coincidence that the prospect of heaven—the alternative to the finality that is dying—receives repeated emphasis.

   Ted Cruz, the one-time Republican candidate for president, appeals to fundamentalist Christianity based, almost exclusively, on reflexive survival instincts, and his support of the ultra-conservative Tea Party with its appeal to those age-old sentiments of that which is old is best, is a clear expression of an unthinking, emotional veneration of childhood innocence. It it easy to venerate those days when survival was a parenting responsibility.

Religions need not be pernicious to survival of the individual, but the failure to exercise integrity—and buying into seductive promises of life eternal in mansions built on golden streets is but one of them—in the realm of self-concept is. We cannot lie to ourselves and be psychologically free.

5. Self-Concept: In this proposed theory of metaphor, self-concept is a metaphor for which humans may take responsibility and, as such, is the one aspect of life over which the individual possesses control. It is, in other words, the arbiter of reality where we may invest consciously in those actions and ideas that make us feel good about our self-created selves—and, in the realm of self-concept (that all-pervasive sense of being), feeling good about one's self is the metaphorical equivalent of survival in the physical world.

Empowered by a positive self-image, and committed to not doing those things that violate integrity, we can take risks, invest in acts of good will, and commit ourselves to making the world a better place, and—at the same time—not lying to ourselves about our real motives. In this better world there is no room for prejudice, no self-serving avarice, no prostitution of another to one's own benefit. And, because we will have constructed our concepts of self responsibly, we can live comfortably independent in our mind—the one region in this world where real freedom is possible.

As opined by me elsewhere, there are consequences to the casual use of metaphor.

6. Art: Those famous cave drawings in Lascaux (see **The Shamans of Prehistory**, Jean Clottes and David Lewis-Williams) feature surrealistic images of elands and bison, remarkable for their power and mastery. Interestingly, when men are portrayed, they are diminutive stick figures sequestered away at the bottom of the drawings. This confirms two things to me— that all art may be traced to the drive to survive—the drawings were magical depictions designed to ensure successful hunting—and that the earliest renditions of self-concept were undeveloped (and are) an evolving thing.

My son's earliest paintings were remarkable for their emphasis on depictions of certain of his physical attributes, his eyes, his nose, his mouth. As his artistry matured, the self turned muted, but until his improbable death of cancer in 2017, his art (and mine) represents an effort to secure the survival of self —not in prizes and profits, but in the memory of posterity, in the dream of creating an art that survives one's death. All art is truly about survival, not of the physical self but of ego.

Poetry (my specialty) is the sublimest of the arts because—excepting in its use of vocal cords—it is less dependent upon physical elements in nature. (That metaphor is best that is farthest removed from physical survival instincts.) This is true despite the fact that nature is art's primary source of metaphor. Sculpture requires marble, painting requires canvas and oils, and music requires notes and physical instruments. Poetry—its progenitors were originally spoken— requires only metaphors, the pure synthetic stuff of idea.

7. What is being proposed here is no minor thing. The philosophy of metaphor contains the wherewithall to redirect the path of humankind. Accepting the fact of our inevitable mortality and avoiding, like the plague they are, those deceptive metaphors that promise us an immortality unconfirmed by experience or science, will empower us to commit our lives to activities that promise survival based on a willed commitment to non-physical survival. Self-empowered and committed to a responsible construction of our concepts of self, we can manifest our lives in the only kind of freedom possible in this life and, in the process, we will have contributed to the creation of a planet freed from the consequences of lives driven by subliminal impulses as old as the hills and committed to nothing but staying physically alive—regardless of the cost to integrity, the planet, or the quality of our human souls.

N.B: It is perhaps worthy of comment than not one of the men in attendance (and they represent the crème de la crème of society as it exists in the archipelagic world that is Brevard, North Carolina) has responded, in any way, to this document. Mayhaps they are self-satisfied?

Grounded Metaphor
An Essay

The following is a twice-rejected critique of a literary explication written by Professor Dan Albergotti of East Carolina University. The poem under discussion is Melanie Carter's "Water to Sky" and, in addition to discussing what I perceive as weaknesses in the Professor's philosophy of literary criticism—to say nothing of the poem under consideration—I define my concept of metaphor and argue for the importance of grounded metaphor in literary criticism and human psychology. Before reading the essay—admittedly pedagogical and esoteric—the reader is encouraged to read excerpts from the poem under consideration on page four below. This essay is significant (in my prejudiced view) for its discussion of grounded metaphor. The reader is reminded that essays (like everything) are metaphors.

— 1 —

I recently had the opportunity to read a poetic explication sent me by a former student. The article was from **Poets and**

Writers. From the following comments, it will be immediately apparent that the professor's perspective annoyed me greatly.

The article in question is entitled "The Truth of Imagination: Metaphor's Universe of Possibilities," by Dan Albergotti: Poets and Writers [n.p., n.d.] and the poem being discussed is Melanie Carter's "Water to Sky." Professor Albergotti writes:

> Carter did not consciously seek out these metaphors, nor immediately perceive their intricate connections. No, such metaphorical apprehension only comes—if we are lucky—through the unconscious mind in the act of composition when we've managed to outwit our consciousness with a pure focus on the senses.

The implication of this statement would seem to be that poetry is an unwilled product of the unconscious, that poetry is a gift within which the writer does not even "perceive" the "connectedness" of her metaphors." Under this scenario, the poet is simply medium and the unity of the poem is a magical coincidence.

As a practicing poet, I can tell you that not only do metaphors *not* arrive from a vacuum but that the intellect is consciously involved in rejecting and selecting those metaphors that speak to his/her poetic issue. Metaphors do, indeed, derive from the unconscious, but they are grounded in the poetic imperative and are at their best when their recognition of "similarity in dissimilars" can be traced back to its originating source—a property delayed for later discussion.

It is telling, to me, that Professor Albergotti has selected "Water to Sky" to support his thesis, for I cannot conceive of a poem based more solidly on the use of ungrounded metaphors. The first instance may be seen in her use of "trimmed," as in the hummingbird having "trimmed" the air. Just what this image is intended to evoke is never made clear to me, though Professor Albergotti suggests that we are somehow expected to deduce fabric being trimmed.

The next instance of ungrounded metaphor occurs in Carter's characterizing the hummingbird as "hardly more than a green seed...." I have a hummingbird feeder outside my sliding glass door, and I have had opportunity over twenty-odd years to view thousands of Ruby Throats feeding at my feeder. Not once have I viewed one with the faintest similarity to a "green seed." To characterize a hummingbird as such is not only arbitrary, it is groundless.

And then, with reference to the bird's red chest, she suggests that it "must have swallowed the hook God dangles into this uncertain sea." Albergotti proposes that through the miracle of metaphor the hummingbird has been transformed into a fish—a contrived happening whereby the metaphor of "God's hook" is somehow justified.

While I admire the metaphor "uncertain sea," I can find in the poem no precise point at which the air turned into "sea," and the idea that the bird's chest (which is red naturally) is somehow transmigrated into blood from "God's hook" is a reach too far for me.

(In a previous life, I was an ardent fisher of rainbow trout, and not once did the barbed flies I used provoke bleeding of any sort.)

For a metaphor to speak to me, there must be some sort of logical progression of events, some basis in real life: a connection whereby the metaphorical connections are made clear. The only logic here is the whimsy of the writer and her quixotic comparisons.

And then, after what is likely the most effective metaphor in the entire poem:

> "...its wings pluck/the invisible line it is suspended from, and the diphthong note that quivers through the air sounds like a fiddle string gone out of tune with all the distance between here and there..."

she jumps, inexplicably, to her dead father "playing this creature, this stunning blood stone, caught and reeling."

This hummingbird, this hooked fish, this chunk of mineral is somehow "caught and reeling." One can only speculate at the reason behind her father's cruelly "playing" this innocent creature, and the use of the term "reeling," raises in my mind the image of a fishing reel, or drunkenness, most certainly illogical extensions.

Of this passage, Professor Albergotti writes,

> Is the creature that's 'caught and reeling' a fish that's been caught and is being reeled in, or is it a marionette caught in its strings and dancing (reeling) for the speaker? Yes, yes, yes, yes. Miraculously, all of it."

To this mishmash of uncoordinated imagery and far-fetched possibilities, I can only respond: No, no, no, and miraculously, none of it! There is no legitimacy in making metaphors into whatever we wish them to be—in abdicating responsibility for providing grounding guideposts—and, when we stray from the germ of meaning implanted in the imagery that is metaphor, we are writing for effect and not meaning—we are, in a word, using the formula that is metaphor—saying that one thing *is* another—to fraudulent ends.

Before proceeding farther, I should make clear that in my use of the term *metaphor* is meant to apply to any comparison, be it image, idea, sentence, or exposition. It derives from the drive to survive—that quantum discovery of particles seeking out and finding compatibilities. The entire Shakespearean opus may be seen, then, as a product of the dramatist's drive to survive and as a metaphor of his life philosophy—even as his tragic opus, **Hamlet**, may be seen as a study of a young man caught in the throes of adolescence seeking the maturity that is self-actualization.

(It is worth noting, in passing, that Shakespeare had to write in scenes of warfare and blood to pacify the "groundlings" in the pit below the stage. This is an early instance of *grounding* a metaphor!)

Thus metaphors are seen here as consolidative—that is, as the letters in a word are metaphors of a sound, as are the words themselves, as are one-on-one comparisons, sentences, essays, plays, novels, so may any work of art be looked upon as a thing entire unto itself. Everything that we can conceive of is metaphor—the very act of thinking is metaphor in action. It goes without saying, then, that I perceive the consolidated metaphor that is "Water to Sky" as incoherent and totally lacking in a central unity.

In order to clarify the distinction I am drawing here—between grounded metaphors and free-floating ones (always a product of unexamined survival drive)—I will argue metaphors may be shown to be made up of two terms (not including the bridge-engine that is verb). And, mind you, I am only talking, here, about the basic structure of metaphor—the bare skeleton of the process. **War and Peace**, believe it or not, is a metaphor, the grounding base of which is Tolstoy.

The first term is *operant,* by which I mean to convey the grounding object upon which all subsequent comparisons are predicated. This object may be a word (a pun), an idea (say, Darwin's theory of evolution), or a natural entity (a planet). Whatever the "object," it must function as the *operant* of the metaphor—the mother lode from which the selected resemblance(s) may be taken.

I mentioned, earlier, that I admired the metaphor of a diphthong note sounding "like a fiddle string gone out of tune..." for "...all the distance...". Despite my objection to "the invisible line," I admire the sonorous sound evoked by "diphthong note" and the metaphor of the fiddle having gone out of tune because of the sound having traveled so great a distance "between here and there"—though, to be honest, the location of "there" had not been established to my satisfaction.

The effectiveness of these two metaphors I trace to the fact that unlike other metaphors in the poem these are grounded metaphors that refer to real objects in real time. Though it was not suggested in the poem, the warning sound a hummingbird makes around the feeder can be aptly described as a "diphthong note," and I find it fetching to conceive of the dissonance in the note to be a consequence of the bird's having "traveled" so far "between here and there...." Furthermore, I admire "uncertain sea," though, again, seeing the air as "sea" is not justified (in my mind) by the use of "hook"—which itself has no grounding referent." No red-throated "fish" could survive in a salty sea!

Unfortunately the readings of the appreciated lines I suggest are provided no basis in the poem as written. This having been said, the metaphors are *still* grounded in the sense I mean. A strummed string *can* evoke a diphthong sound, and a fiddle string may *actually* go out of tune from slackness. The metaphors can be seen, then, as deriving from real objects in a real world, and applied to a hummingbird they enhance the image of the bird.

Thus seen, the bird could function as a richly invested *operant* for a powerful *denotator*. In this poem, the *denotator*—"My father must be playing this creature/ this stunning bloodstone, caught and reeling..." comes across as abrupt, arbitrary, and as totally unprepared for in the context of the poem's *operant*, the hummingbird.

Based, as the poem is, on ungrounded metaphors, the metaphor that is the poem itself must be seen (in my eyes at least) as ungrounded and, therefore, open ended. It can mean what the reader wants it to mean and I, for one, have no coherent idea of the meaning Ms. Carter intended. If, as the open-endedness of her metaphors suggest, she is accepting metaphors unselectively, as they bubble up from the unconscious—an exemplification of what I have termed an unexamined expression of survival drive—then she is engaging in the premeditated use of ungrounded metaphors.

Excerpts of the fourteen-poem follow:

Water to Sky

For seven days a common hummingbird
has trimmed the air outside my window.
Hardly more than a green seed, it glides
from pane to pane presenting its fine throat—
a fragment so soaked through with red I think
it must have swallowed the hook God dangles
into this uncertain sea. Is it wrong to say God?
Because when this bird moves, its wings pluck...

From my having the subject of grounded metaphor on my mind as a result of reading "Water To Sky" and writing this essay, it is not surprising that during a recent reading of the **Scientific American** magazine (July, 2011), I came across several excellent instances of what I call grounded metaphors (an illustration, by the by, of the way metaphor seeks out and finds connections!) in Lee R. Kump's article, "The Last Great Global Warming." The following three instances are instances of grounded metaphors. They are: "methane belches," (p. 59), "left on the counter to thaw," (p. 59), and "planetary fever," (p. 61).

Since methane is viewed by scientists as one of the major causes of global warming, and, since in this context it bubbles up from the ocean, it is not difficult to see "belch" as a *denotator* with direct linkage to its *operant,* methane.

The metaphor "left on the counter to thaw," builds on the author's description of permafrost being like "frozen hamburger in the freezer"—also, by the way, a metaphor with direct denotative linkage! He refers to permafrost (as a result of thawing) as being "essentially left on the counter to thaw." Here the *denotator* is the phrasal expression, "left on the counter to thaw," and the direct linkage is to the operant hamburger—also a metaphor of permafrost, and a grounded one at that!

The third metaphor, "planetary fever," has as its *operant* "planetary," and the word *fever," (the denotator)* conveys the senses of both heat and illness.

All three metaphors are highly effective, and one reason for this may well be that in each case the *operant* is a physical entity that possesses clear and direct linkages to its *denotator*. *In* other words, the metaphors have integrity because they are true to their source, their *operant*. *They are* not open-ended and therefore subject to any interpretation.

This is most certainly not the case with the metaphors found in "Water to Sky"—a title, by the way, with no "grounded" connection to the poem itself—like "trimmed the air," "a green seed," "the hook God dangles," and (though it pleases) "the uncertain sea." So obscure are these metaphors that the reader is literally freed to assign any meaning that pleases. Since no guideposts to meaning are given—no honest guidance provided for seeing a humming bird as a seed (and a green one at that!)—the writer, I contend, has written a poem that fails the test of metaphorical integrity. Her metaphors cannot be seen as connected to a solid referent, an *operant*.

— **2** —

At the risk of digression (or worse, sermonizing) it is important to point out that self-concept is—like a poem—a metaphor, and building one's self-image out of a conscious determination to be honest in one's dealings with the world is to *ground* one's self in the reality of real actions in a real world, and it is, furthermore, the grounding of that integrity necessary to a responsible creation of that person's sense of self. It is, in other words, imperative that we abjure ungrounded metaphors ("If it feels good, do it.")— those kind of actions are ideas generated by unconscious metaphors concerned with our physical gratification only, *id est*, survival.

We may not save the world by being honest with our metaphors (though the journey of a million miles begins with the first step), but we will most certainly live responsible lives, recognizing that the consequences of not living true to ourselves are inevitably self-doubt, irresponsibility, and—most tragically—a stupor-driven life in which a witless servitude to survival drive is our only human portion.

Thus a self-sufficient sense of self—a product of personal choices no one else can take credit for—can make possible a grounded sense of self not based on (or dependent upon) public perception (a bona fide instance, by the way, of ungrounded metaphor!)—that kind of self-perception where one feels good about himself/herself on the basis of a perceived reflection in the eyes of others.

A realized concept of self is sufficient unto itself, and public applause is for the needy.

Should this argument for grounded metaphor have value—if our metaphors are consciously made and based on honest connections—its implications are monumental, extending far beyond the issues of rhetoric, poetry, and pedagogy, and extending its fingers into the warp and woof of society itself, its religions and sociology, and even into that most important of metaphorical enterprises, human psychology.

The use of open-ended metaphors, whether they be actions based on impulse—ideas that serve the end of an unquestioned drive to survive—or poems that use the metaphorical formula for an ill-gotten or illusory certainty—is dangerous. That way lies hypocrisy and the death of all integrity.

With a plea for reader tolerance and forgiveness for a degree of self-aggrandizement, I end this essay with a poem about a butterfly—written by me and providing, I hope, an instance of grounded metaphor.

Blight

A phantasy of light and wing
A child crushes at play,
And crying home
Beseeches that
The stain be wiped away.

So, man who slays a lovely thing
Weeps not the beauty banned
But dressed in sack
And ashes grieves
The smudge left on his hand.

Let's Talk Turkey

The following three essays are selected from a now-dormant blog originally designed to define and demonstrate the role of metaphor in our lives.

Aristotle made a mistake when, in **Poetics,** he limited metaphor to rhetoric. That he did so is understandable, given that Quantum Mechanics was yet over two thousand years away, but the fact is that limiting metaphor to language—as important and essential as human communication is—has blinded us to the fact that everything in nature is traceable to metaphor.

When Aristotle proposed that a metaphor says one thing IS another, he was right. What he didn't know is that when one subatomic particle recognizes affinity in another particle—a process that, like all metaphors, involves comparison—it said, "let's get hitched." And so it was that those two particles united and, in effect, became "another," an object that had never existed before.

From this initial comparison, and driven by the need to repeat the process, all forms of matter derive. This drive—and my term for it is survival drive—is the force behind all planetary motion, the changing of the seasons, the swinging of the ocean tides, and the propagation of all living things—yea, even the falling of an acorn in autumn-time.

But metaphor and evolution (one of metaphor's most important products) were not done with us. Not content with the creation of inorganic and organic matter, not satisfied with its many forms of reproduction and its successful propagation of species capable of surviving in the venues of air, water, and land, survival drive extended itself onto yet another plateau—this time, the world of mind.

All living things have brain—be it the most miniscule of cells, Eric Kandel's sea snails, or a silver-backed gorilla—and all brains are dedicated to one end, survival—procreation and survival being synonyms. Brain is the organ of survival, the biological incarnation of survival drive.

And while it must be said that all living things have brains, it does not follow that all living things have self-concept; and it is the evolution of self-concept enhanced by language that makes possible that most important of survival metaphors, the human concept of self.

Just where the line of demarcation lies between that most rudimentary concept of self (represented, for instance in Dr. Paul McLean's male rainbow lizards' loss of radiance when defeated) and that most elevated form found in humans,

I cannot say with any certainty. This, however, I can say: Self-concept is a metaphor with important ramifications for survival in the realm of psychology.

Not just Whistling Dixie

In an earlier blog I opined as how self-concept has important ramifications for survival in the realm of self. I propose, now, to discuss some of these so-called ramifications.

First, however, it might be useful to review some terms. The drive for survival, for instance, is the force that drives all creation. The means by which it achieves this end is through the act of metaphor—that comparison force that seeks out affinities, be it in elementary particles, physical and biological matter, or in psychology as construed in the term, self-concept.

Survival remains the issue behind all molecular and psychological structures, and all metaphors may be traced to it. When particles find affinity and become a new and different entity, for instance, the discovery is experienced as survival initiated and accomplished. When affinities are found in a red, red rose and in the concept called love, we experience the same aha! response, an affirmation that is the signature of metaphor found and survival accomplished.

(That the metaphor has its root origin in the similarities between rose and vagina is [perhaps fortuitously] no longer remembered.)

As already stated, self-concept is a metaphor constructed, over time, by the survival relevance of experienced events. Ann Faile broke my heart in college, and I judge all romantic possibilities by the criterion of that pain. My mother's love—so intense, so powerful, so controlling, so suffocating—was such that even today I find myself measuring my accomplishments against "what would mother think."

Self-concept, then, is a metaphor constructed over time by events and circumstances, some of them unnoted and yet influential in the self we perceive.

This self perceived by each of us—Do I like myself? Am I competent to survive in a dog-eat-dog world of competitiveness, favoritism, and chicanery? Am I worthy of love? Do my friends respect me, honor my opinions, and seek advice from me?—is far more powerful than is generally perceived.

The degree to which we respect ourselves exerts enormous control over the choices we make, the person we choose to marry, for instance, the risks we are prepared to take, the nature of our friendships, our church affiliations, and even our political perspectives.

Feel like the world is going to hell in a hand basket, that morality is dead, that Christianity is under siege, that God will have to erase the human race for goodness to survive? Be a Baptist!

Feel threatened by the obstacles to "making it," feel that the cards are stacked against you in promotion possibilities, in money-marketing accounts, in bailing out banks too big to fail, and by politics? Join the republican party!

Feel all the world is looking for a handout, that what most people want is something for nothing, that nobody cares about hard work and amassing sufficient capital to live independently, that government is the problem, not the solution? Join the Tea Party!

Now, admittedly, these examples are slanted and mirror my religious and political views, but, pause for a moment and look at them for evidence of survival force.

The first example supports the saving sentiment of survival beyond the grave; the second deals in physical survival as measured against money and politics; and the third instance promotes the paranoid view that almost everybody, but you, is shiftless and out for self.

While these examples come no where close to exhausting self-concept formations that condition the way we live our lives, they do highlight the role played by the unexamined (reflexive) drive to survive—in the ways we construct our concepts of self, and in the ways this impulse may condition our outlooks on life and the choices we make.

The point is this: Either we will develop our concepts of self reflexively—based on life experiences and the way we reflexively interpret them—or we will do so consciously, by learning to examine our metaphors, taking responsibility for them and the actions based upon them, and by consciously choosing not to be motivated by instinctive survival drive.

(If god is in charge of our decisions, then building self-concepts reflexively is divinely sanctioned.)

Self-concept, it must be said—as predicated by the parenthetical statement above—can be created by delegation, ie, unconsciously, or we can choose to purposefully create ourselves—utilizing the metaphorical mechanism of conscious and responsible construction of self-concept—and bequeathing to ourselves, thereby, the wherewithal to do good, to build sculptures, to paint pictures, to write plays and poetry, to care for the poor and disadvantaged, for our environment, and to propel ourselves into a better future on the wings of a higher form of survival—actions of will, consciously formulated, that free us from reflexive survival drive, liberating us to create those things that survive our dying and that leave behind a world better for our having been here.

Our physical bodies are essentially vehicles designed to facilitate physical survival, but our concepts of self are what make us human. We can, in other words, invest in those actions and ideas that make us feel good about the self we perceive. We can abjure those that don't.

When I say that self-concept is a metaphor with important ramifications for survival in the realm of psychology, I am not just whistling Dixie!

Responsibility for Self Begins at "Home"

In "I'm Not Just Whistling Dixie" I posited the theory that not assuming responsibility for one's metaphors has serious implications for the state of one's psychological well-being. In this blog I propose to present a prescription for taking on this responsibility. "Home," as the quotation marks are meant to indicate, lies in the mind of the individual.

The statement that follows has been variously attributed to Vladimir Lenin and to the Catholic Church: "Give me your children until they are twelve years of age, and they will never depart from our teachings."

I don't know if Lenin or the Church ever made such a statement, and whether one of them (or both) did, is not for me, a matter of pertinence. What does matter, however, is the seemingly arbitrary selection of the age of twelve.

It is no coincidence, I believe, that this age is (or at least used to be—before hormones and antibiotics became the panacea of choice to pig farmers)—the typical year for the onset of puberty, the time when young people are mandated by the maturity of their reproductive organs to come to grips with their sexuality.

This quotation appears to me to be based on the conviction that if children have been properly conditioned (by church or state)—brainwashing is a lot easier when brains are malleable!—then the odds of controlling behavior are a lot better. It is not, in my view, a state to be aimed for.

Whether or not this was the underlying motive of the quote, it is my contention that the onset of puberty marks the time when blossoming adults are mandated by nature to confront the issues of sexual identity and sexual choices. It is also the ideal time to introduce them to the concept that self-concept development is a personal responsibility.

While it would not be inappropriate to introduce these concepts earlier, according to the philosophy of Comparison Psychology—my proposed approach to balance in the world of mind—it is at this point of maturity that parents and teachers should begin teaching young people how to accept responsibility for construction of self-concept.

Furthermore, it is believed, parents should structure opportunities for their offspring to make choices as conscious investments in feeling good about themselves, and parents should accept the fact that conditioning a child's behavior to suit their personal views of how people should live their lives is the ultimate act of selfishness and personal pride. It is the concept of slavery applied to mental emancipation.

In this proposed approach to the psychology of self, parents would recognize and children would be told that building a positive self-concept is their responsibility, and that their choices and performance levels are building blocks to self-sufficiency—a state of being that will determine character and the levels of success they will know as adults responsible for making their own way.

Allowing children to suffer the consequences of failure is the first law of parenting and an act, on their part, of genuine love. While it is permissible to ask, "What did you learn from this? How will your response to it contribute to your building a responsible sense of self?" it is not acceptable to be judgmental or to threaten consequences. Sufficient unto the day is the self-punishment thereof.

Along with parents, teachers bear an awesome responsibility for self-concept development. Not only must they teach their subject matter—preferably without such punitive coercions as grades—but theirs is the responsibility for teaching real-world consequences. They are not the biological parents of the student—"love has nothing to do with it"—and their job is to educate, not cuddle.

Not only is the student's mastery of subject matter conducive to a positive sense of self, failure to do so is a failed opportunity for self-enhancement. A properly designed system of education would allow students as many opportunities for subject mastery as their levels of ability require. Artificial markers such as grades and grade levels would be abolished. The goal, after all, is self-enhancement, not the application of standards meant to stamp the student as inferior in the eyes of self or peer.

I am one who favors year-round school—it is the height of foolishness to allow expensive facilities to languish empty and unused for three months out of a year!—but I would like to see one semester out of every year in high school dedicated to a self-esteem camp/laboratory where students would be provided opportunities to make positive investments in their sense of self. The opportunities could be adjusted to skill level, and students would learn at their own speed —with no tolerance for judgment or criticism—but failure to succeed would not be an option.

In addition to opportunities for conscious self-enhancement provided by parents and school, the world is replete with opportunities for individual investment in the positive construction of self, and students should know that the choices they make are crucial. Among their available choices are how they will choose to respond to the challenges of peer relationships, to choices about illegal drugs and dress, to decisions about sexual conduct, birth control, choices (or non-choice) of religious beliefs, of personal values, and how one wishes to contribute to society, to ecology, to science and the arts.

They should know that the choices are theirs and the consequences real. The opportunities are there; however, the will and know-how may not be. That is role of responsible parenting and teaching. Advice may be sought, but the right to choose is inviolate, the consequences inevitably their own.

Someday the world will come to recognize that everything we perceive is metaphor—that we can fashion our self-concepts reflexively—subject to the whims and vagaries of primitive survival urges and happenstance—or we can build them consciously, examining and controlling our motives, being— to steal a slogan— "all that we can be."

We need not be slaves to primitive survival impulses, and we owe it to our children—if not to ourselves—to grant them the freedom of responsible choices, choices that will empower their personal freedom.

We are, whether we like it or not, the people we choose to be.

Self-Concepts Choices:
Illustrative Vignettes

What follows is an attempt to illustrate the role of metaphor in adolescence, that period where the business of self-actualization assumes a dominant role in our lives. These "vignettes" are taken from a revived version of my original blog, a compilation now dormant as well. The characters depicted here are fictitious and any similarities in the lives of people known to me are strictly coincidental. Jackson Stewart is a pseudonymous avatar for me.

— 1 —
Mary's Story

Mary was fifteen and preparing for entry into her freshman year at the local high school. She was nervous, imagining at night when she couldn't sleep all manners of encounters awaiting her: She would fit in easily, have lots of friends, and take on minor leadership roles in her freshman class; she would be ostracized and left standing alone and unnoticed, a country mouse pushed out of the way in hallways full of jostling students; or she would be seen as mildly attractive but imminently unnoticeable.

She and her mother had spent hours in the shopping malls, not just looking at clothes, but observing closely what other teens were wearing. And, though her mother was interested and supportive, she was absolutely unhelpful. Mary had a problem. She didn't know how she wanted to appear to her classmates, but she absolutely didn't want her mother telling her who to be.

Did she want to wear jeans and a fringed shirt, looking comfortable and just a little bit hippie? Did she want to appear suave and sophisticated, risking the label of preppy? Should she be Hollister, Gap, Abercrombie Fitch, or Old Navy? And shoes were a problem—did she dare wear boots, long or short?—as were hair style and fragrances. Even though they were all the rage, she still felt uncomfortable with the thought of jeans with pre-engineered holes and frazzles.

And then there were boys! Up to now, her parents had limited her dating—if it could be called that— to group outings to matinee movies or to holiday parades, always with the stipulation of absolutely no pairing off. But, now, restrictions were off, and finally she would be allowed actual dates—with a real-life boy, going to honest-to-god movies, to pool parties, and, with luck, maybe even to Senior Prom.

From the issue of boys and dating, her mind flowed to questions of sex, drugs, and birth control. Both parents had seen to it that these issues had been discussed in detail, and she knew very well what their position was. She was committed to their point of view because it was safe, but she also knew she hadn't been tempted yet.

"It's easy for them to say," she exclaimed to herself. "They think it's just a matter of laying down rules and my following them exactly! They have no idea—or else they've forgotten—about the importance of being liked, having honest-to-god, real-life friends; and they've forgotten all they ever knew about how like hell it is to be thought of as weird or out of touch with what's really going down."

"It's too much of a hassle," she exclaimed. "I think I'll just settle for home school!"

— 2 —
Marc's Story

Marc was fifteen and had played football in middle school. He hadn't exactly warmed the bench, but he was certainly no Friday-night hero. He doubted he'd be invited out for varsity, and he wasn't sure he wanted to be in any event.

Marc was in love—so much so that he'd come to question just about everything in his world. He'd just gotten back last week from a Christian camp at Lake Toccoa where he'd met Annette. Her skin was chestnut brown, she wore her hair long and black, and, in accordance with her tanned skin, was possessed of chestnut eyes as big as playhouse saucers.

At first she hadn't seem to notice him—she seemed obsessed with Oliver Martin, the friend he'd come to camp with—but Oliver ignored her completely. Finally, though, she smiled at him in the lunch room, and soon they were taking walks after dinner—always chaperoned, of course—by the senior counselors lagging, conspiratorially, behind.

That night, when he finally got up the courage to hold her hand, blood rushed in torrents from his heart to his hands, he felt a deafening humming in his ears, and the world seemed to take on a decided slant. They had never kissed, and when they hugged that one time, as she was boarding the bus back to Monroe, it had been a stiff embrace, bodies bent awkwardly askance so as to avoid touching. Upon arrival at home, he had messaged her immediately about his feelings, his unfailing loyalty, and the beauty of her moon-like eyes. The idea of sex—and its being the reason for the humming in his ears—never even crossed his mind!

She had not replied, but it had only been a week. He'd just have to be patient. In the meantime, his mother was all agog about his starting high school, about clothes, back packs, and notebooks, pens, and pencils. He couldn't care less. His heart (and mind) belonged to Annette!

— 3 —
Suzanne's Story

Suzanne was fifteen and entering her freshman year at Drucker's Senior High School. She was not nervous, for this would be her fourth new school in the past eight years. Her father, a colonel in the Air Force, was subject to reassignment every time he got promoted, and his transfer to Drucker, WVA., represented his first stateside posting in seven years. She was looking forward to being American again, and getting some homegrown relationships.

A tall girl, approaching six feet but not there yet, Suzanne had red hair, a sprinkling of freckles skipping across her nose and cheekbones, and she was decidedly beautiful—although to her great disappointment her breasts were embarrassingly undeveloped. Her hips and backside, she opined, made up quite satisfactorily for those deficiencies. Feelings of inadequacy, while common, had not taken up permanent residency!

She had already made preparations for her first impression. She would appear at Drucker's dressed in tight-fitting slacks, a glamorous blouse with compensatory purple ruffles, tall boots, and a French beret slanted rakishly across her tightly curled coiffure. She expected that guys would trail her down the hallways like hound dogs tracking a raccoon, and she would address them condescendingly in one of the four languages she spoke without accent.

Suzanne—survival drive alive and thrumming—was primed and prepped, ready for action.

— 4 —
Mary's Story Continued

Mary had seen to it that her mother deposited her at Drucker's High thirty minutes before the opening bell. She wanted time to check out the facilities, to mentally map out the location of the offices, the double-lined classrooms that branched off the central hall, the location of the lockers, and all the building exits. She read, for the umpteenth time, the curriculum assignments, school rules and regulations, and the mapped-out location for each room assignment.

She was determined to be ready for anything.

The issue of dress had been decided for her by the picture of a model she's studied in **Cosmopolitan**, so she felt good about the way she looked. The dark brown slacks fitted her perfectly, and the light tan blouse with its high collar she'd selected all on her own cradled the round features of her face and gave off the impression of the lost young waif she was aiming for. Her hair, permed and cut short by the stylist she had waited two hours for, nestled just inside her collar. She wore hardly any makeup, and her lips were a light-tinted pink. She was, she thought, as ready as she could ever be for the comparisons—male and female—she knew she would have to face.

The first person to walk in the door at the north end of the hallway was—wouldn't you know it!—Marc McClanahan, the next-door neighbor she'd known almost all her life. He was nice enough, but big-feet clumsy, and his teenage acne rambled like splotches of crab grass across the mask of his broad-grinned face.

She forced a smile and held out a limp hand in response to his high five.

"Hello, Marc. Nice to see you again. Where've you been all summer?"

"Been away at summer camp, but thank God you're here. I was sure I'd see nobody I knew. Do you feel as lost as me?"

"I'm nervous, excited, too. It'll be great to meet new people."

The two young people leaned nervously against the wall and observed the students now filling up the hallway. Both of them wanted to find a better place to stand, but neither of them knew how to separate.

And then, right before their eyes, she sauntered past—her red hair flashing ruby highlights from the florescent lights on the ceiling, her high-heeled boots tapping our a message of cocky confidence and fearlessness, her wide green eyes focused on some certain spot midway down the hall. Suzanne had made her entrance!

— 5 —
Marc's Story Continued

It had been three and a half weeks, and still he had not heard from Annette, and, though he had twice visited with Oliver—playing competitive billiards on his father's table— and had brought up her name once or twice, hoping he would have some insights, Oliver had remained stubbornly non-committal.

He turned, now, away from Mary and looked around the hallway for Oliver but caught no sign of him. Oliver, he knew, had attended the camp for years and was well-acquainted with all the regular campers, and Annette, Oliver had mentioned, was one of them.

He turned his attention back to Mary.

"Will you be taking college prep?" he asked. "My parents insisted I sign up for advanced Algebra, and I can't tell you how scared I am!"

"Yeah," Mary responded. "My parents are determined I'm going to college, too. Maybe I'll see you in Algebra," she said, easing her way down the hallway in the direction of the wall lockers.

Marc, aimlessly picking at the straps of his backpack, watched her walk away. He found himself comparing her to Annette— her medium height, her somewhat pale complexion, and the straight-forward way she walked, no swaying hips, no consciousness of being looked at.

Annette, on the other hand, had the look of a gypsy about her, and her hips moved as though in cadence to an invisible tambourine.

"Oh, yes! She knew she was beautiful."

Maybe that was why she expressed no interest in books or attending college. Her interests revolved around social things: who was dating who, who was rumored to be having sex, and whether so and so's parents were illegal aliens.

Ordinarily, Marc might have been bored by such trivialities, but Annette's lips were luscious, and she had the kind of eyes you could dive into and gladly drown in the depths thereof. He was, of course, totally oblivious to the real source of his feelings.

He wished she would respond to his phone calls and messages. Maybe her phone was down, maybe she hadn't received his messages; maybe he should try to tweet her. He instinctively knew, however, that appearing too interested could be seen as an admission of weakness—though weak he was, he ruefully conceded.

He was startled from his reverie by the five-minute bell and strode off down the hall in the direction of home room. As he entered the door, he bumped against Oliver who, lost in thought, had not left room for sharing the entrance way.

"Well, hello, buddy!' Oliver exclaimed. "I hope your pool game has improved. Either your mind wasn't on the game, or you've lost the knack."

"There ARE advantages to having a pool table in your basement," Marc rejoined. "I'll skunk you next time!"

"And, by the way," Marc continued, trying hard to appear casual, "Do you by any chance know Annette's mailing address. She hasn't responded to my messages."

"I don't know, Marc. I might have it some place at home. I'll look for it, if you want. My advice, though, is forget about her. She's not into long-term relationships."

"I know you've known her a lot longer than I have, but I really thought we had something going on.

"I hate to tell you, Buddy, but what you had going on was her trying to make me jealous. We were together once—I don't think I ever told you this—but she's not a one-man kind of gal. She tried this summer to tell me more than once—even sent me messages by other campers—that she'd changed her mind, that I was the only guy she'd ever love. Well, you know what I say to that: Burned once avoid the fire!"

Marc stared at Oliver, slack-jawed and drained of color,

"You've g-got to be k-kidding me, man!" he stammered, grabbing Oliver by the shoulders and looking him hard in the eyes. "I thought we were friends, that you'd tell me anything, that you'd never try to hurt me."

"Marc, I wanted to tell you, a dozen times. I was just hoping it was a summer fling for you. I never thought you would dive off the deep end the way you have. I'm sorry, man; and you are my friend, the best I've ever had. But, take it from me. You won't be hearing from Annette Rodriguize."

Marc shoved his way past Oliver and stumbled to the back of the class room. There were tears, unwelcomed, in his eyes.

"He just had to be wrong about Annette. They had felt too much together—when they touched, their shoulders had melted together like butter!—for it to be his imagination. Maybe it was Oliver that was jealous! He'd not give up so easy. If necessary, he'd hitch-hike to her house this coming weekend. A love like theirs was for eternity!"

— 6 —
Suzanne's Story Continued

Suzanne was nonplussed that, so far, no one appeared to have taken notice of her. She was leaning against the white board, carefully centered, her beret rakishly slanted over her forehead, her right elbow cocked on her jutting right hip, her eyes fixed in a somewhat jaundiced stare at the spaces between the clustered students waiting, like her, for the final bell and seat assignments.

It was home room, and she knew exactly nobody.

She was taken aback, therefore, when a mousy little girl—dressed, appropriately, she thought, in brown—sidled up to her and introduced herself as Mary.

"I saw you in the hall, first thing this morning," Mary exclaimed. "You most certainly are not a native Drukerian!"

"Whatever a Drukerian is, I certainly am not!" Suzanne huffed. "I transferred here from the Ecole Francais in Paris. I've never seen such pandemonium! Where on earth is the teacher?!"

"He will be here shortly. I'm sure," Mary responded. "I'm enrolled in French, freshman year. Maybe you could tutor me, at the soda shop down town—my treat?"

"Not likely, I'm afraid. I expect to be busy every day after school in that equestrian class Pa Pa signed me up for. From the looks of you, though I can't imagine you'll be needing any tutoring. You look like the studious type."

"I am in honors classes, and I always come to class prepared; but that doesn't mean I'm not interested in new and different things, and you are most certainly both of those! You could have just stepped out of a fashion magazine. Since you're new to Drucker, I'd be glad to show you around?"

"We'll see," Suzanne demurred. "But here, at last, is the honored professeur!"

"Settle down, people!" Jackson Stewart yelled. "Take any desk. I'll assign seats as I take the roll. Welcome, freshmen, to Drucker High!"

"Not too bad looking, for a southern hickster," Suzanne murmured appreciatively, shoving an intervening body aside to take a seat in the front row. "Maybe I won't be bored out of my mind, after all!"

— 7 —
Mary's Story Continued

Two weeks had passed and Mary's school life had settled into routine. She liked all her classes and had found none of them too challenging. Even beginning French had turned out to be easy—doubtlessly due to all that hard work she'd done studying English grammar. Still, though, she had made few friends, none of them close. She'd had high hopes for Suzanne, but that saucy gal from Paris had little time for her. Seemed like she was always chasing after Mr. Stewart, asking him questions and doing her flashing-lashes routine.

"She's such a flirt!" Mary exclaimed to herself. "You'd think with all that European sophistication she'd know better. Just wait until she sets eyes on Mrs. Stewart, all grown up and beautiful."

Mary, then, was very surprised when Suzanne called to her on her way to study hall.

"Wait up, Mary. I'll walk with you!"

Mary waited, dubious as to the redhead's motives, but intrigued nonetheless.

"I didn't know you had study hall today," she said, smiling."

"Don't usually," Suzanne replied. "But today my riding class was canceled—something about a horse show in Mayview. I thought maybe we could visit that old-fashioned soda shop you mentioned, after school. And I'd be glad to answer any questions about French."

"Actually, turns out French is going pretty well, but I could probably use some help with accent and pronunciation."

"It's a date, then. I'll see you there! You need a ride?"

Mary responded affirmatively, making a mental note to message her mom, and watched as Suzanne flounced her way between the desks and to the back of the class room where she swooped into a desk, crossed her legs with practiced grace, and opened a book Mary thought likely to be a novel, not a textbook. She opened her cell phone and messaged her mother about not needing a ride.

"I wonder what she could possibly want of me. Certainly not dating advice!"

Suzanne was waiting in the student parking lot when Mary exited the building, and her tap-tap-tap on the horn of the red convertible attracted Mary's attention immediately.

"What a great car!" she exclaimed. "It's French, isn't it?"

"Nope," Suzanne responded. "A Miata. Pa Pa bought it for me on my sixteenth birthday. It's a guy magnet, don't you think?!"

"I'm not sure I'd call it that. It's more of a golden chariot!"

"What it is is an invitation to a speeding ticket. I've learned to drive it very, very carefully."

Inside the soda shop—Drucker's tribute to a by-gone time, to stools and booths and teenage servers dressed in flouncy, peppermintery skirts—the girls ordered milkshakes and examined the posters pasted on the walls. There were posters of a young Elvis Presly, a dapper Dean Martin, of Doris Day dressed in gingham, and other long-gone-and-unremembered stars of a forgotten time.

"What I wanted to talk to you about," Suzanne said in a hushed surprisingly muted, voice, "was about you and me being friends. I'm having real problems getting to know people here, and you're so intelligent and so accepted by everyone. I thought maybe you could help me out, tell me what I'm doing wrong."

"You flatter me!" Mary responded. "I've just lived here forever. I know how to live up to expectations."

"I thought these West Virginia boys would flock to me. I haven't even had a date!"

"Join the club," Mary chuckled. "I know lots of guys, but not one of them has asked me out, or even flirted. I could set you up, though, with my next-door neighbor. He's nice enough, but nowhere near to being anywhere in your league."

"What's his name? And what's he known for in school?"

"Marc. And I believe he's on the football team. But as far as his being known for anything, I can't say what it would be. He fell in love in summer camp, and she shafted him. He's still pretty broken up about it."

"So, I get him on the rebound. That's all right with me. I'm desperate to escape the house, and, who knows, maybe he could introduce me to the quarterback!"

"I'll talk to him," Mary promised, accepting the tall milkshake from the peppermintery server and placing a napkin under the steel tumbler holding the leftover, milky remains. "If this doesn't add padding to our posteriors, nothing will!"

— 8 —
Marc's Story Continued

Oliver had been right. Marc never heard a word from Annette. He'd poured out his heart to her, given himself up totally. Well, never again! He had decided, instead, to try out for football, to pour his energy and misery into practice and the weight room. With most of his life still out ahead of him, it was stupid to get so serious about women.

Unbelievable they would stoop to playing games like that, turning men into objects for their own purposes!" (The irony of that statement went unnoticed.)

And he had to admit, the exercise had made a difference. Not only had his acne disappeared, his neck size had increased, and his biceps actually bulged from the sleeves of his tee-shirt. And he'd made the team—first string!—been moved from left end to defensive safety.

When Mary stopped him in the hall yesterday, he'd remembered his comparison of her with Annette and thought how out of his head he was back then. It seemed months ago! And then it occurred to him how seldom he thought about Annette any more, how much, how quickly, she had become a forgotten chapter. Back then he would've sworn his feelings were recorded in cement.

Maybe Mr. Stewart was right that you can only know what you know based on what you know!

Mary had commented on how much stronger he looked and gracefully forgot to mention his heartbreak.

"Have you met Suzanne Wittington," she asked. She's new to Drucker—attended school last year in Paris, France?"

"I've been so busy with practice, I've not met anyone not on the team!" he said. "Why'd you ask?"

"She's been having trouble meeting people here—people see her as a snob—which she sorta is. But she's really kinda nice when you get to know her. We've gotten to be friends, and I mentioned you to her the other day. She said she'd like to meet you."

"I'm not sure, Mary. After Annette, I'm not much into the dating thing. Maybe, though, we could meet at lunch, in the lunch room. Could you arrange it?"

"For sure! You eat at 12:00, right? We'll see you then."

Being on the football team gave students additional benefits where food was concerned, and Marc piled his tray high with extra beef dogs and corn bread. He also took an extra slice of apple pie and a large iced tea.

"All that exercise puts on extra appetite, if not weight," he commented to himself, picking a vacant table near the exit and looking around for Mary and her fresh-from-Paris friend. He noticed them immediately, wending their way through the scattered tables and crowds of milling students.

"Marc, this is Suzanne Wittington, the girl I was telling you about. Suzanne, this food disposal unit—pointing at the heaping plate before them—is Marc Morgan."

Marc stood, held out an embarrassed hand to Suzanne, and said, "I thought, Mary, we were friends! And you talk about me that way. I get a lot of exercise, Suzanne. I need to eat!"

"Com' on, Marc. You gotta know I was kidding! I'm proud of you, making the football team and all that," Mary said. "To say nothing of those new muscles you've put on. Not only that, you're making As in Algebra!"

"So far, at least," Marc responded, holding two chairs, somewhat awkwardly, for the two girls. "It's nice meeting you, Suzanne. How're you liking Drucker?"

"Well, it's certainly not Paris!" Suzanne replied. "But I do like that retro soda shop. And Mary's been really nice to me. School's been something of a drag, though."

"I identify!" Marc responded. "I'd be bored out of my mind if it weren't for football. Are you into any sports, Suzanne?"

"Mary may've told you. I do the equestrian thing, thanks to my father. But I'd like to know more about football. When do you play again?"

"Next home game is two weeks from Friday. I could get you a front-row seat, if you are really interested. Mary wouldn't be caught dead at a football game!"

From there the conversation drifted smoothly from friendly gossip to discussion of favorite songs and types of music, and current movies. To Marc, the hour seemed to have wings. The meal over, he collected the trays and walked between the girls to the exit.

"See you later, ladies," he joked, emptying the trays into the garbage cans and stacking them neatly on the counter by the door. "It was really nice meeting you, Suzanne. Thanks, Mary, for introducing us."

Marc had no inkling of how carefully Mary had tutored Suzanne in toning her assertiveness down and in not dominating the conversation. He was pleased, over all, with how the meeting had gone.

— 9 —
Jackson Stewart Comments

I have been a teacher of English at Drucker High for going on four years and have had opportunity to observe the three students profiled here in both home room and in class.

Mary is an excellent student, mature for her age, and likely to be a scholarship candidate at a major college. Marc is likely of above-average ability, but his involvement in football has had an impact on his academic studies. Coach says he shows great potential. Suzanne is a product of a military family, has traveled widely over two continents, is consequently very sophisticated (flirtatious even!), and seems to be undergoing problems adjusting to Drucker backwardness.

Based on these observations, and with the advantage of having read the above-referenced profiles, I would now like to propose an approach to education meant to facilitate the conscious development of self-concept in adolescents. I've shared my approach with the principal and other teachers, admittedly to little effect.

The first observation I would make is how insignificant are the roles parents play is in the presented vignettes. The parental influences may well be significant, but adolescents are, by and large, either oblivious to them, or terrified of their peers seeing them as being under their influence. Almost without exception, their emphases are on how they are perceived by their peers—likely, I suspect, a consequence of physical survival drive applied obsessively to ego.

This emphasis is understandable in that high school freshmen are ostensibly on their own for the first time. Parents and their teachings may be important in subliminal ways, but it is apparent that "out of sight, out of mind" is the dominant *modus operandi.* As stated: The dominant adolescent emphasis (and this is regrettable) is on such survival issues as sex and how they are perceived by peers.

Mary is perhaps the best indicant of this premise—with her emphasis on clothing, hair style, etc.—but Suzanne has obviously put considerable thought into dressing to impress.

As presented, Marc seems oblivious to these issues, but this is largely a product of his obsession with Annette and his sublimated sexual impulses. It is apparent, even so, that he is very conscious of bodily appearance and takes some degree of pride in his improved physical appearance.

My first point of emphasis is that an absorption with acceptance is a sign of a still-developing concept of self, evidence of the absence of ego security that comes with confident self-knowledge. Parents have little or no influence in this realm since one of the first issues of adolescent independence is making one's own choices as to self-image, and level of peer acceptance, perhaps the paramount factors in the individual's self-view. Parents, besides, are universally seen as ancient and uninformed.

(The lack of a realized [and presiding] sense of self may explain the ease with which many adolescents are persuaded to experiment with drugs and unprotected sex. A school-wide emphasis on the individual's responsibility for self-concept might go far in eliminating or reducing susceptibility to these kind of temptations.)

Adolescents, I have observed, are cursed by their being driven by nature to grow up as quickly as possible. The fact is they can only know what they know, and the result is that they often make life and death decisions based on insufficient evidence—an inevitable consequence of limited time on the planet.

Were teachers sufficiently educated in the ramifications of my theory of metaphor—in how survival information is stored in modules connected to synapses geared to blindly seek out connections—and how the fewer the modules the less likelihood there is for viable connections—they might be better equipped to persuade their students to delay important choices based on the fact that the fewer the modules they have the more likely they are to suffer consequences based on their limited experience.

Adolescents, however, are notoriously suspicious of adults, and persuading them of anything requires providing them opportunity to connect with and relate to an adult they can trust—trust being the ground stone on which all successful pedagogy is based. This accomplished—and education ought to be placing emphasis on the importance of consciously constructing one's self-concept, not on the basis of competitive strategies personified in numerical grades, class ranking, and parental status—it becomes possibly to educate students on self-concept responsibility. Self-concept is, after all, the predominant factor in human achievement.

I believe, further, it is possible to persuade students that relying exclusively on the perceptions of others is the death knell to self-sufficiency. Stress should also be placed on the consequences of failure that accompany (and indemnify) an insecure self-concept. Success is built on confidence, and confidence is the earned consequence of self-concept responsibility.

In addition, under the system proposed here, students would be encouraged to recognize that academic success—far from just providing the oft-touted assurance of viable employment opportunities—provides opportunities for practicing self-concept responsibility, for feeling good about themselves, and, most importantly, for exercising integrity in personal decisions and relationships.

Students can be taught (and encouraged to accept) the concept that they, and only they, are responsible for self-concept construction—that no one, parent, dating partner, preacher, or teacher—can do this for them—that theirs is the consequences of failure to make necessary investments in an earned sense of self.

Stress should be placed on the demonstrable fact that the quality of self-concept contributes to the levels of success they achieve in life, financially and psychologically, that their taking responsibility for the quality of their images of self can have practical benefits not only in their minds but in society as well. More importantly, they need to understand that adhering consciously to self-selected standards can "buy" them contentment in the realm of self, the freedom to be who they choose to be.

A second observation regarding the above profiles is that for whatever reason two of the characters in the above scenarios are adjusting well to the challenges presented in their initial opportunity for independence. Mary is well on her way to constructing a stable concept of self. She is a good student, an astute observer of her peers, and a person bent on making her own decisions. Though she indicates its importance to her, she is obviously not obsessed with finding a guy. Unfortunately, she does not—nor has she been taught to—see her actions and ideas as conscious investments in building a self-sufficient sense of self, a lesson that would doubtlessly accelerate her success.

Marc, as indicated in his summer-camp experience, has not been educated in the ways survival drive expresses itself in sexual attraction, its most common manifestation. He obviously would have profited from instruction in distinguishing the difference between lust and love. (His insight into the surface issues Annette perceived as important probably accounts for the relative ease with which he escaped his infatuation.)

Even so, he is to be commended for his decision to invest in football and physical conditioning instead of dwelling on Annette and his broken heart. That he is feeling better about himself is evidenced in the disappearance of his acne, his developing physique, and his success on the football team. He is even making As in algebra! Like Mary, however, he has not been taught to see these accomplishments in terms of a conscious investment in self-concept, a consequence born of an improperly focused pedagogy.

Suzanne's destiny is uncertain, and this is despite her worldly experiences, her knowledge of languages, her considerable potential, and an over-indulgent home environment. Her carefully studied self-image actually derives from the same insecurities that bother Mary and Marc. There is room for thinking that her penchant for flirtation (resorting to the utilization of primitive survival impulses) comes from a self-concept not constructed by conscious investments in self-esteem.

It is likely that the successes she envisioned have not happened because of her self-image having been so obviously created for effect. Her insecurity comes across as snobbery and, doubtlessly, other students than Mary had noted her flirtatious ways.

Her most positive attribute is her willingness to accept that her approach to life at Drucker High is not working and that she is willing to consult Mary in hopes of changing. Just how sincere her efforts at reformation are remains uncertain, however—as evidenced, perhaps, by her off-handed comment about quarterbacks, indicating a too-easy acceptance of the role of status in relationships.

Finally, it is apparent that none of the teens has been educated to the undercover modes of expression played by survival drive in their thoughts and actions. Part of the blame may be placed on the parents (who are themselves uneducated in survival subterfuges and not likely to know that self-image is a metaphor engineered for survival of the psychological self.)

Emphasis on this function of survival drive could be used to reenforce responsibility in the realm of self-concept.

As stressed throughout this proposal, survival drive may be seen as first metaphor, the comparison force that drives matter—both real and virtual—to seek out affinities. As the original force behind the formation of matter, life, and self-concept—since the appearance of homo sapiens—its repercussions are most apparent in the actions undertaken in an unconscious protection of self-concept.

At the risk of over-emphasis, I must stipulate again that it is to the metaphor that is self-concept—an evolutionary development responsible, in this writer's opinion, for the importance of separateness, particularly in the human individual—that we trace the origin of language, of counting, the art of writing, of science, and—ultimately—the creation of art in all of its amazing manifestations.

It is to this invention of self-concept, as well, that we trace the human's awareness of mortality, the subsequent need for gods, heavens, religions, and their notions of survival beyond the reach of death. All metaphors, it can be seen, are traceable to the drive to survive, and personality (one's concept of self) is no exception.

While it is important to re-emphasize that a responsible development of self-concept provides humankind with its only means to freedom—freedom existing in the mind or no where at all!—it is imperative that students be taught that the concept of self is subject to reflexive construction—as a consequence of instinctive response to circumstance and experiences, thought not being given to why or wherefore.

Untested and unthreatened, blessed with a secure physical environment, with loving and supportive parents, and a genetically assured high I Q, possessors of self-concepts engineered by happenstance could conceivably glide through life uninfluenced by the concerns that motivate Mary, Marc, and Suzanne—to say nothing of what happens to teens exposed to soul-scorching poverty, abuse, and abandonment, and to a multitude of other shocks and arrows human flesh is heir to.

It comes down to this: Threats to physical survival trumps every other survival issue.

And this must be said: Possessors of auto-conditioned self-concepts are unlikely to care anything for the state of their peers or the conditions of the poor and mistreated on the planet; and it follows, therefrom, that it is to these individuals that most instances of bullying may be traced; and it goes without saying that these individuals—energized by appeals to their primitive survival motives—might actually elect a president or even a dictator.

Since these individuals' sense of self is created reflexively—by programmed religions and/or unexamined survival impulses, their everyday concerns are likely to be built around issues of physical survival. More importantly, however, is the soul-scorching reality that they may be forever trapped in the machinery of an unquestioned survival drive, that they will never know the ecstasy of being truly alive and psychologically free.

Self-concept is the one entity on the planet that can be consciously constructed with an eye to the good of self and of humanity. It's downright shameful that the world—and especially our institutions of learning—are blind to this possibility and responsibility.

Attached is a copy of my proposal sent to the West Virginia State Board of Commissioners for implementing metaphor into public education.

Strategies and Implementation: Self Concept and Education

— 1 —
Reforming Education

It is because of the importance (and universality) of education in society, and based on my observation that it is in high school that students are first allowed the opportunity for making their own decisions, that I suggest the need for a redesign of secondary education structured around self-concept development.

As suggested in the vignettes, it is during these four years that students are first confronted with the real-world business of deciding who they will be; and it is at this time that their personal responsibility for self-concept creation must be driven home. Education should see to that.

As envisioned, the first step in this proposed redesign of secondary education would be the movement to year-round schooling. The school year would be divided into four semesters with students (and teachers) being allowed a semester's sabbatical of their choice. Students could elect to attend all four sessions as means of accelerating graduation, but students not living up to expectations (not completing research projects satisfactorily) would not be allowed the option of a semester off—a real-world inducement to assuming responsibility for responsibly developing one's sense of self.

My second design change would be elimination of all numerically based grades. Grades are an artificial device for measuring intellectual aptitude, based most often on an autocratic assessment of what kind of learning is best. In my experience, they are more important to the teachers than they are to the students—though academically talented students often utilize them as a means of self-demarcation and as testament to their superiority. A gradeless system would attenuate these possibilities. Moreover, as suggested earlier, the academic curriculum would present immediate, real-world opportunity for conscious investment in self-concept.

Success, responsibility of the individual student, would be the product of joint (teacher and student) evaluation, an assessment measured by effort and actual accomplishment, not numbers based on subjective evaluations. (Self-concept, after all, belongs to the student—not his teacher or educational institution!)

My next proposal involves one-on-one instruction made possible by the ubiquitous personal computer. Students would be assigned individual study carrels (rather than classrooms) and would conduct research-based projects under the careful supervision of an assigned teacher. Memorization would be discouraged, and students would be encouraged to seek out practical applications for what they learn. They would also be allowed—within the constraints of decency—to decorate their carrels according to personal taste. Dress codes would be eliminated, but "Health" classes would emphasize the consequences of revealing outfits and pretentious clothing (being unconscious expressions of primitive survival drive) to the development of a responsible sense of self.

While the lecture method may be utilized, it should be used sparingly, and primarily as a discussion-based exercise. Grades (Pass or Pending) would be assigned based on the status of self-determined individual projects, and students would be allowed as many opportunities to succeed as needed to feel the affirmation that comes from earned accomplishment.

I would also suggest changes in curriculum. One of the first changes would be making mandatory a class on self-concept construction. This class could be called "Health," but its primary emphasis would be on discussion of self-concept and on how it is each person's responsibility to develop—through responsible choices—a positive sense of self. Self-criticism would be welcomed and encouraged, and negative comments or sarcastic laughter positively forbidden. The course would be required all four years and should be designed so as to demand greater effort and creativity each year. Every senior would have developed expertise in word-processing during their four years and would self-publish a project based on their chosen area of academic interest.

— 2 —
Philosophical Bases

Social relationships—including the issues of peer pressure, smoking, the use of drugs, and dating—are exceedingly important during the periods being discussed here. These issues would be emphasized in "Health" classes as opportunities for conscious investment in a positive sense of self. Failure of students to live up to their self-created standards of behavior, they should understand, would inevitably lead to defective (ineffective) self-concepts. In other words, they will have invested, by choice, in failure. Imperative, here—in interest of avoiding the very whiff of intimidation—would be an emphasis on self-concept being a self-directed enterprise.

Being "good" because of external pressure—whether from parents, teachers, peers, or the legal establishment—would be presented as coercive and, therefore, not conducive to the construction of a positive sense of self. Free will is essential to responsible choices, and the conscious, responsible use of it (and the rewards that come from it) would contribute to a positive sense of self.

Successes in the core curriculum—English, Social Sciences, Mathematics, and Science—would provide students with the opportunity for positive contributions to self-concept construction. In fact, no student would be allowed the escape-clause of failure. In addition to the core curriculum, students would select courses in the fine arts, or in practical, work-experience courses like auto/body/auto repair/ maintenance, drafting, construction, animal husbandry, and agriculture—all subject to published standards of success (affirmed and graded by students) and dedicated to construction of the student's concept of self.

While failure would be avoided at all costs—to the extent possible even the assignment of "Incomplete" would be kept confidential—students would be held to the highest possible standards of accomplishment. No student would be subjected to instructor criticism, and all disciplinary issues would be handled by the teachers responsible for "Health" classes, in coordination with the parents of the offending students. Students could choose to plead their cases before a jury of their peers, half of it made up of students selected by them.

Under terms of this proposal, the function of administration would be truncated. The offices of principal and vice-principal would be eliminated and replaced by a dean of instruction; guidance counselors would be eliminated in favor of the teachers assigned responsibility for "Health" classes. A business manager, charged with responsibility for finances and the maintenance of buildings and grounds—including the school cafeteria—would be employed. Paid (work-study) positions would be available to all students.

The office of records would be updated, with emphasis placed on the protection of documents and the inviolate privacy of student records. Only assigned teachers would be permitted access to student records/documents, and this access would be limited to specific classes taught. Students would have unquestioned access to their records and encouraged to appeal perceived discrepancies to the dean of instruction.

Under Research and Development, an annual report on innovative projects and results, as well as comparison studies with other cooperating school systems, would be prepared and disseminated by the dean of instruction, and proposals for new projects would be encouraged—from faculty and students.

Referrals to colleges and universities would be handled by the dean of instruction, in liaison with the student's instructors over the years of attendance. Follow-up surveys on student progress would be conducted at colleges and universities, and efforts would be made to continue relationships with all graduates. To this end, successful graduates would be honored by appearances at student assemblies and invited to speak.

School publications would be uncensored and produced solely by students, with the positions of editors limited to graduation candidates. An adult adviser to publications would be assigned, but this person's role would be limited to issues of format and the mechanics of spelling and grammar. Controversies about content would be referred to the dean of instruction and a selected student panel.

Parental concerns (and it is expected that they will be many) would be brought before a panel made up equally of students and teachers and headed by the dean of instruction. Irresolvable conflicts could be adjudicated by the county superintendent of education and/or the county commissioners.

Appeals of local decisions could be taken to the state department of education and the standing governor. Under terms of this proposal, rulings based on paternalistic interpretations—that parents and parents alone are responsible for the upbringing of their children—would be strongly discouraged. Students do not ask to be born and are not the property of their parents.

Finally, taxpayers will provide funds necessary to the construction and management of a museum and/or gallery for preservation and presentation of student projects selected for purchase by a committee made up of students and faculty.

— 3 —
Athletics and Self Concept

Under terms of this proposed remodeling of education based on self-concept, athletics would play an important role in self-concept development, one justifying their being addressed in this separate section. This emphasis is warranted because of the close (and ancient) relationship between metaphor and action—success in hunting by our ancient forebears, for instance, undoubtedly led to the earliest expression of self-concept—and this connection contributed to the factor of grounding in metaphor, a crucial aspect of effective metaphor. (For an extensive treatment of this aspect of metaphor see:

Metamorphosos: A Proposed Path to Independent Living,
pp. 255 ff.)

As envisioned in this application of athletics to self-concept development, coaches would perform no other functions than coaching and would be responsible for no more than two major sports. It is anticipated that—as is the case with academic courses—all sports activities will be directed toward self-concept enhancement. This means that students not capable of performing at appropriate levels because of physical disability will be trained by rehabilitation experts in individual instruction designed to enhance physical capabilities. Progress would be the only criterion of success.

The value of sports (team or individual) is that they provide immediate feedback in the translation of mental concepts (metaphors) into real-world affirmations. In other words, an athlete envisions an act—a gesture—and proceeds to make that vision a reality. The result—taking place in the actual world—provides direct input into the concept of self, in contrast to academic studies where delayed gratification is often required.

Sports, then, take place in a physical world, as is not always the case in academics, and are, possibly, the most direct conduit to that metaphor that is self-concept—as are, by the way, all eventually successful reproductions of metaphor, be they physical or ideational. Unfortunately, as bodies age, athletic metaphors become harder to actualize, with the consequence that self-concepts built up from athletic accomplishments are subject to loss of potency, and, as a consequence, we see former successful athletes attempting, again and again, to return to arenas of past success.

Ultimately and ideally, self-concepts should be constructed of more enduring substances—things like academic accomplishment, positive responses to effective parenting—and upon being graduated—to professional success, and honest-to-god contributions to society and posterity. Art has been long established as one of the world's most enduring metaphors.

It can be said, then, that athletics (because it involves comparison-based competition) may be seen as a necessary evil—since in contests there must be losers and winners. This said, learning to accept one's inadequacies (despite maximum effort) can be helpful in its own right, and the conscientious application of effort (performing to the best of one's ability) contributes immediately to construction of a positive sense of self.

Not everyone can be successful in all things, but all human beings have areas in which they can excel. This means that students not blessed with effective athletic genes can always find their "self-reenforcing talent" some place else and succeed there. Abetting this discovery in their students is, of course, one of their teacher's most important responsibilities.

It should be apparent, by now, that achievements of physical goals (accomplished in a real-world context) can contribute meaningfully to a student's accepting responsibility for his/

her concept of self. The self-concept, after all, is a mirror of the physical self, and a well-conditioned body (its upkeep being the responsibility of its bearer) is essential to it.

— 4 —
Concluding Comments

The metaphor that is self-concept is not an amorphous entity. It is real and clearly the most important agent in survival of the psychological self. Furthermore, research indicates that how people feel about themselves has significant chemical consequences, that positive self-image contributes to physical well being, and that good self-concepts lead to positive consequences in real-world activities. Dedicating the educational process to enhancement of self-concept is not, therefore, an illogical or impracticable concept. There is meat, I insist, on the bones of this proposal (note metaphor!).

And, while it is recognized that positive self-concepts are not built in a day, and that utilization of the public schools does not address all students and every opportunity for positive investment in self-esteem, it is held that adolescence is the ideal point to take on the process of responsible self-concept development.

Because not every student in every situation could be addressed under terms of this proposal, every opportunity should be taken to involve parents and leaders outside the academic community in holding students to the strictest possible standards of responsible performance. The philosophies advocated for here are clearly equally applicable to private academies and charter schools.

Successes (social, academic, or athletic) lead to confidence, and confidence leads to quality performance. Under this proposal, it is predicted that parenting will be greatly simplified, communities will be enriched, and employers will be assured of qualified employees who work not only for money but for pride taken in every endeavor.

And it is true, of course, that real-life failures (whether in school or community involvement) may be used as "teaching moments" to prepare students for those inevitable failures that happen in a molecular world, aided and abetted by human bosses geared by inadequate self-concepts. Learning not to take personally the inadequacies the inadequate inflict is one of the vital first steps to developing a competent sense of self. (It is, of course, helpful to self-concept development to learn [and practice] tolerance for the inadequacies of others.)

Learning to confront and correct inadequate performance (whether in academics, athletics, or people relationships) is the key to construction of a self-concept sufficient to the tasks of living and living well.

Historically, the educational system has been viewed as the cultural melting pot where students could be conditioned (brainwashed!) so as to further the end of good citizenship. This said, it should be said here, that standards of good citizenship (such as they are) are arrived at by a consensus metaphor that bears more indebtedness to physical survival drive than anything else.

This has got to change, and the proposed restructuring outlined here (subject of course to study, experimentation, and necessary revisions) would go a long way toward eliminating the ambiguity of the present system, would put the educational emphasis on the individual student—making for the development of good human beings rather than citizens—and hold society responsible for a responsible education of its citizenry.

It is often said that the future of a country rests in the hands of its youth. Implementation of this proposal would go a long way toward assuring that the future of our country rests in good hands indeed!

The Tyranny of Ungrounded Metaphor

"...people only believe the news is credible when it neatly dovetails with their own beliefs."

John Boyle, AC-T, 11/20/16

The above quote is taken from a column by John Boyle, a columnist with the **Asheville Citizen-Times,** that deals with the issue of fake news—a phenomenon receiving particular notice during the 2017 election season. Fake news— abjuring the current President's definition and practice— is prefabricated news based on the writer's desire to secure converts to his/her point of view. The quote is cited as an example of the way "ungrounded metaphors," referenced in the title to this essay, may be engendered by the character of self-concept.

I define ungrounded metaphors as reflexive tropes motivated by the drive to secure survival of the psychological self, a reflexively constructed metaphor driven by the desire to survive—physically and psychologically. I call them ungrounded because they are predominantly reflexive and, in most cases, not based on facts derived from study, research, or scholarship. They are commonly found where fear—whether rooted in bigotry, racism, or religions, and/or political fanaticism—predominates.

The results of the last Presidential Election—election of Donald J. Trump, and republican majorities in both houses of congress—would seem, based on results, to add credence to the theory of ungrounded metaphor proposed here. Certainly, analysis of the characteristics of voting majorities suggests that white citizens, and particularly non-college-educated ones, turned out to vote in unprecedented numbers—a consequence, I contend, of a calculated appeal to the most primitive of survival instincts.

Among these basic instincts appealed to were expressions of overt racism (support for President Trump from the KKK and use of the phrase "good people on both sides," for instance), the invocation of Nazi salutes at meetings of at least one so-called Alt Movement, and the vehicular assault of a protester in Charlottesville, VA.—to say nothing of repetitive verbal assaults on Jews, Mexicans, and Muslims—strike this writer as equally suggestive of blatant appeals to subliminal survival instincts.

This said, I find myself pulling back from a popular conviction that poor whites vote against their own best interests because of racism. According to my philosophy of metaphor, racism is but one of many expressions of the reflexive drive to survive—in this case, growing out of the need to feel comfortable psychologically by "taking the easy way out"—by acceding, unthinkingly, to the reflexive character of their self-concept.

The National Rifle Association, with its emphasis on weaponry, I argue, is impelled by the same unexamined drive to survive—as are many members of the far right coalitions in the U.S. Congress.

As indicated elsewhere, and implied in the title of this piece, metaphor is the unrecognized mechanism behind all creation—from comparisons made in nature, to scientific discoveries, from the invention of languages to the creation of fiction, non-fiction, and philosophies, including religions. As stipulated, all metaphors are based on the drive to survive, first physically, then psychologically.

It behooves those of us intent on surviving thoughtfully to heed the moral imperative of survival on our own terms—otherwise freedom is an impossibility.

Metaphor, and this is illustrated in the metaphor that is the theory of evolution, began simply and adapted, over time, into more complex—more efficient survival organisms. The human brain, for instance, began as a cellular reflex and ended up as creator (and metaphor) of a physical (and non-physical) world.

The universe began, then, as a physical thing, something as simple as a cell endowed with a need to seek out affinities. Over uncountable eons—and it is important to note that time itself is metaphor and, as such, had all the *time* in the world to seek out, reject, and try again all possible combinations of the substance that is matter, allowing, thereby, its survival and advancement—adopted advances being another word for survival efficiency.

This physical universe was grounded (pun intended) in matter, and survival was a pragmatic fact—either the formula that was metaphor worked on matter or it didn't. When metaphor turned non-physical—i.e., containing the unforeseen consequence of idea—the pragmatism of material combinations no longer applied, and fiction became a possibility.

(This said, it is important to note that metaphorical efficiency is made possible in metaphor's original reliance on matter, the source of its invention and the *grounding* factor in the equation that is comparison.)

The highest accomplishment of metaphor, so far, has been the metaphor that is the human self-concept. This evolution was doubtlessly the consequence of self-evaluations growing out of physical consequences—the best spearman was the best hunter, etc., etc.—and soon there were priests, individuals with the self-built authority to transport us to heaven and eternal survival, the ultimate antidote to the ultimate infamy—that infestation of our genes called mortality.

Albeit an ungrounded metaphor—lacking a basis in human experience—survival now had wings!

Self-concept begins anew with each newborn infant, with the in-bred need for food. This need evolves to the need for comfort, the need for love, and ultimately to the need for survival (feeling good about oneself) in the psychological self.

This metaphorical progression can be interrupted at any point, with significant consequences to the developing sense of self. Parentage is obviously important, and good parenting is imperative. There is (or should be) more to the process than inseminating an ovum.

This said, it must be stipulated that there is much more involved in self-concept development than parenting. Ultimately, each individual is responsible for the character of personal self-concept, and it is conceivably possible, to develop a concept of self based on purely instinctive responses to physical stimuli. It follows that an individual who based self-image on responses to physical survival impulses alone—assuming that such a thing is possible—would end up psychologically stunted.

The metaphor that is self-concept exists, of course, on a spectrum, extending from expression of the earliest (most primitive) survival impulses to such metaphorical constructs as bridges, computers, self-concept, and works of art. Modern metaphors—be they inspired by physical survival impulses or by psychological ones—are likely to be efficient and more conducive to survival, be it physical or psychological.

Metaphors derived from self-concept (bridges, computers, self-concept) suffer from Huxley's pathetic fallacy—the ability of the unprincipled to lie by attributing ungrounded qualities to idea—as illustrated, for instance, in fake news. The "news" lacks grounding in fact, research, and documentation.

Examples of ungrounded metaphors in the context argued for here are easy to come by, but I was particularly impressed by a metaphor published recently on the obituary page of a local newspaper—an interesting irony, given the promised survival-beyond-the-grave emphasis of most obituaries! The advertisement follows, with relevant passages italicized:

> A raindrop landing on your cheek is a *kiss* from someone that *lives* in *Heaven* and is *watching over* you.

A raindrop is a creation of nature and typically means what it means. When it is called a kiss, however, the raindrop becomes a metaphor—one ungrounded in fact or human experience. That the *kiss* comes from someone that *lives* in *Heaven* and is *watching over* you—all ungrounded suppositions grounded on faith (itself an ungrounded metaphor based on feeling) —illustrates, as well, the physical survival emphasis typified in reflexive metaphors.

Adding to the irony is the ethical quandary of the newspaper consciously appealing to instinctive survival drive in the interest of making money. Refusing to cater to reflexive instincts is the essence of a morality based on the assumption of responsibility for one's concept of self.

Similar issues are raised by the passing of collection plates on Sunday and in the publishing of essays for money—one of the factors involved in this writer's abjuration of marketing in general. The fact is, however, that the execution of metaphors for the furtherance of physical survival is legitimate—else how could roads be built or babies fed?

The answer to this question may be found in another question: What kinds of activities ground our metaphors, and which do not? It is obvious that the obituary metaphor lacks grounding in nature or in fact. And those metaphors promising survival in another realm in exchange for money, share the same fallacy.

Roads secure physical survival of the workers involved in their construction, are paid for by taxes collected (hopefully) in the public interest, and are grounded in the facts of commerce, communication, and convenience. Babies, while not asking to be born, contribute to survival of the species and to feelings of competence derived from responsible parenting.

Ultimately, metaphors are grounded in action—actions taken in the interest of self-concept. Individuals so driven—and contributions made to the elimination of poverty, to housing for the poor, for climate protection, and the welfare of humanity in general are grounded metaphors all—are empowered to do good, are unflustered by insecurity born of ungrounded metaphors and the consequent feelings of inferiority, and are free to invest unabashedly in the construction of a confident sense of self.

There is no biblical vanity here. On the contrary, an individual empowered by the knowledge of history, by love of the arts, by a dedication to the betterment of the human race, and by a commitment to being the best human being possible cannot help but advance the cause of humanity.

There is no greater metaphor, one grounded in the betterment of all.

The Gordian Knot Untangled

*The following "essay" is excerpted from **Metamorphosos: A Proposed Path to Independent Living**, my ponderous (and some would say prolix) exposition of metaphor and its role in the development of humanness. It is quoted here in the way of summation to this collection of essays. In this chapter subtitled "The Gordian Knot Untangled" I have utilized the semi-parasitic shrub, mistletoe, as a metaphor of metaphor—suggesting through it a solution to human "cannibalism," itself a metaphor of the endemic conditions underlying our failure to finally fulfill our quest for Edenic bliss. (Bracketed passages indicate editorial additions.)*

In the work referred to above, I have proposed that the miracles of art, music, science, and literature are living examples of what is possible through the willed transmutation of primitive survival drive into conscious self-concept metaphors.

It has been implied (if not said) that our survival as a species depends upon our assuming responsibility for the still-evolving metaphor that is self-concept.

One perturbing question remains: What is there in us that compels us to kill and eat our gods?

It is a question, apparently that bothered Sir James Frazer as well. In his prodigious catalog of survival metaphors, **The Golden Bough** (op. cit. **Ibid.**) he proposed at least three answers:

1. Common sense decreed the god be killed before he became old and feeble.

2. Survival-of-the fittest contests assured the survival of vegetation in a "less delapidated tabernacle";

3. The primitive mind conceived of holiness as a "sort of deadly virus" the prudent man would do all he could to avoid.

In addition to these hypotheses, Sir James discusses the paradoxical "crowning and killing" of the "final harvester"— the least-swift reaper of the grain—as a more human way of sacrificing the god.

Each of his possibilities, the reader will note, can be directly related to issues of physical survival.

These explanations leave me unsatisfied—because, perhaps, they leave human beings in the same sad state he found us at the beginning of his work.

Even so, it is with thanks to Sir Frazer's artful identification of Aeneas's golden bough as mistletoe that I would like to propose an answer more compatible with my thesis of survival through the conscious use of metaphor.

It has been stated that everything on this planet feeds off everything else—it is the method of comparison—and schizophrenia was presented [in **Metamorphosos**] as a radical instance of this in the realm of self-concept.

This inherent cannibalism—the fact that in order to live we must eat, to survive we must kill—may even have, it has been suggested, something to say about the universal con-taminant, guilt.

Is it possible that to the primitive mind mistletoe served as evidence of something that survived without feeding off something else? It was, after all, found on the tree of the gods (the oak), it was rootless, and it stayed forever green.

(It has only been in modern times that we have found out its parasitic secret, and even so its hold on us remains so powerful that we continue to kiss —a prelude to coition and physical survival?—our lovers under it!)

The oak is wounded by the bolt of lightning, the yule log burns that we may enjoy warmth and good fortune, the virgin bleeds that humans may be born, the corn god dies that we may feed, and we still devour the Eucharist.

If, indeed, It should be this paradox that governs so much of our unconscious lives—that gives lie to our most deeply revered pretensions, that forces the recognition (and the sublimation) of our innate cannibalism, then it becomes understandable why we persecute the final harvester and why the scapegoat market flourishes even today.

It is at once the curse of life (could Abel have been such a sacrifice?), a symptom (if not the cause) of eating disorders and schizophrenia, and the origin of guilt? Is it true, we kill and eat our gods that we may live?

In a proposed solution to the problems suggested in these questions, I would like to suggest that in the sought-for perfection of self-concept humans may find the psychological equivalent of mistletoe—something that needs not eat its god, a non-carnivorous construction built on the sound foundation of taking responsibility for one's own synthetic self.

(That, even under this scenario we must eat to survive physically, is mitigated by the hope of future scientific discoveries. Soon, very soon, we will make our food from unbleeding particles snatched from the air and combined— through the act of metaphor—into whatever kind of food we desire!)

It is an audacious thing I am proposing, but should there be value in it, one small thread shall have been unraveled from the cord that binds us all, living and bleeding sacrifices on the altars of our own careless construction.

Freed from the serpentine embrace of our fear of death (and its psychological twins, insanity and guilt) we just might empower ourselves to brush aside the forfending scimitars at the gates of Eden and re-enter—as titans at last!—the symbolic lands of our ancient origins.

Consummatum est!

Printed in the United States
By Bookmasters